BEYOND THE RAT RACE

BEYOND THE RAT RACE

GLEN MARTIN

BROADMAN
& HOLMAN
PUBLISHERS

Nashville, Tennessee

4261-51
0-8054-6151-5

Dewey Decimal Classification: 155.9
Subject Heading: Stress (Psychology) \ Burnout
Library of Congress Card Catalog Number 95–6451

Unless otherwise noted, Scripture quotations are from the Holy Bible, New International Version, copyright © 1973, 1978, 1984 by International Bible Society. Other versions used are the KJV, King James Version; NASB; New American Standard Bible, © the Lockman Foundation, 1960, 1962, 1971, 1972, 1973, 1975, 1977, used by permission; NKJV, New King James Version, copyright © 1979, 1980, 1982, Thomas Nelson, Inc. Publishers; and TLB, The Living Bible, copyright © Tyndale House Publishers, Wheaton, Ill. 1971, used by permission.

Library of Congress Cataloging-in-Publication Data

Martin, Glen, 1953–
    Beyond the rat race / by Glen Martin
      p. cm.
    Includes bibliographical references.
   ISBN 0-8054-6151-5
    1. Success—Religious aspects—Christianity. 2. Christian life—Baptist authors. I. Title.
BV4598.3.M37   1995
248.4'861—dc20   95–6451
                                CIP

1 2 3 4 5 99 98 97 96 95

Table of Contents

To those who have run alongside of me in my personal Rat Race and cared enough to point out to me the warning signs that have become the essence of this book.

• Dr. Gary McIntosh,
who will always be my lifelong friend and confidant;
who has been there to pick me up when I have struggled
(Eccles. 14) and to cheer for me when I have achieved.

• Mr. Preston Smith,
who saw me, not as who I was,
but as who I could become in the Lord;
who challenged me, inspired me, and motivated me.

• Miss Joy Bell,
who stayed on earth long enough
to draw me into the ministry I love so much;
who was called home when I was called.

• Mrs. Jean Davis,
who cared enough to type and edit and
retype my first manuscript;
who has modeled servanthood to me.

• Miss Dian Ginter,
who has been my family's prayer intercessor for years,
who is always available when my family needs her.

• Nancy,
my wife and best friend,
who has always demonstrated 1 Corinthians 13 love;
who loves me enough to point out
when I am trapped in the Rat Race.

• Kerry, Scott, and David,
my kids, who have put up with the long hours,
long trips, and long prayers of their dad;
who have modeled for me
the grace and acceptance
of my Lord.

PART ONE

Ready, Set, Race!

Chapter One

The Dilemma

"Like a rat in a maze, the path before me lies. And the pattern never alters, until the rat dies."[1] Everyone can identify with such thoughts. Life is not a straight road with no turns nor hidden parts. Without God to shine His light on the road, we can easily get sidetracked, confused, and lost—just as lost as a rat in a maze. Is it any wonder we have come to call a hectic life the "Rat Race"?

WHERE DID IT ALL START?

I am convinced that the human race has always been involved to one degree or another in the Rat Race. We may have used other terms for it, but bottom line, life is a series of decisions, pressures and circumstances that each individual handles either well or not so well. Poor Noah had his version of the Rat Race when he had to build an ark he'd never seen before and then had to prepare all the "fixin's" for dinner for every species of animals of the world—not just for one meal, one day, or even one week, but for 221 days![2] I'd call that pressure. Noah must have been thinking, *Have I forgotten anything? Will this thing float, let alone carry all this weight? And how in the world am I going to get it to the water once it is built? What about the smells and the noise? Will we run out of food and water? What if I really am not hearing God? Am I only thinking I hear Him?* And in the midst of this activity, he felt ridicule from everyone but his family—and we don't fully know how they responded. Yes, I'd call Noah a candidate for the Rat Race. But you can trace the Rat Race even further back than Noah.

How about the first parents, Adam and Eve? Think they might have felt some pressure? Guilt increases pressure. Wonder if after the Fall they ever yearned for the days when they had no knowledge of good or evil and they walked in delight with their Lord in the Garden of Eden, feeling no undue pressures. Surely the enemy must have reminded them of those day as they looked at the slain body of innocent Abel.

As Adam sweated to earn a living—toiling long hours to make the ground yield a living, he well might have cast his mind back to the pre-sin days when there were no weeds, no difficulty in bringing forth the bounty from the earth. Yes, there was work, but it was so satisfying then. As Eve delivered her children in pain, her mind must have flashed back to the reason why such a joyous moment was so painful—her own sin!

Undoubtedly the Enemy must have taunted Adam and Eve with disparring thoughts about how they ruined everything through their sin. Pain, the never-ending weeds—they never could catch up with all the work. Pressure was on all sides, but Adam and Eve did survive.

TWENTIETH-CENTURY VERSION

The Industrial Revolution may seem long ago and far away, but in fact it adds a significant contribution to today's Rat Race. Before electricity, we worked long hours, but we went to bed early because the work couldn't be done after dark. We may have gotten up with the sun, but at least we had a good amount of sleep. there was no television nor movies to watch, no late parties to attend, or cars to take us out at night. The family lived, worked, and played together, so there was seldom that frantic pressure of needing to spend "quality time" with each other. In fact, who ever heard that concept until the twentieth century?

The Industrial Revolution was both a blessing and a curse at the same time. While our lives became easier, they also became more complicated and hectic. The more goods that were produced, the more we felt the pressure to buy. The more there was to do, the more we wanted to take time from other concerns to do those things. Still today, modern society puts our sense of balance on overload. We get caught up in doing, being, and owning, and we become trapped in a Rat Race to try to meet all the unnecessary "needs" we allow ourselves to have.

Indeed, today we have designed our own special Rat Race with pressures that are unreasonable. We never can be released apart from the Lord helping us to reprioritize our goals and simplify our needs. There are two things that are never satisfied, two things that cry out "More, more!" The need to rise to a higher position in work and the desire to own more things. Never can you get saturated, never can you be satisfied.

The person who has chosen to let the world set the standard for how he is to live and has chosen to get into a high-pressured, extremely demanding occupation is trapped in the Rat Race. The thesis of this book is that people caught in such a fruitless lifestyle have forgotten that no one has ever had lasting peace apart from a relationship with God, which includes centering their lives around Him and His will for their lives.

When God is allowed to set our goals, when He is brought into the decision making process as we choose which road of life to take, which profession to pursue, where to live, what to buy, when to buy it, and the myriad of other decisions that are part of the Rat Race pressures, then He can help us order our lives according to His leading. He can point out the pitfalls, show us how to avoid any traps or detours—yes, even set our feet on the right path if we have lost our way from His perfect path.

The chart on the following page gives a quick overview of how the Fall of Man has impacted humanity. The mindset that has developed in man since the Fall gives the Rat Race syndrome opportunity to develop and entrap people unless they have Christ as Lord of their lives.

So let's look at the Rat Race in detail and see why people caught in the Rat Race stay in it.

FIVE REASONS WHY PEOPLE STAY IN THE RAT RACE

In a simple poll of American adults, more than half of the people interviewed shared that they would like to move to the country. Yet three-quarters of all Americans still live in the city. Why the discrepancy? What keeps people away from the lifestyle they want? And what prevents them from making a move? There are five distinct reasons why most individuals stay in the Rat Race.

ANALYSIS OF HUMAN BEHAVIOR SINCE CREATION

AREA	PRE-FALL	AFTER FALL	GOD'S RESTORATION
Dependence	God-dependent	Self-dependent	Dependent totally on God and His guidance.
Self-Image	Good self-image founded in God and the relationship with God.	"I"-centered, need constant reaffirmation.	God-centered, based on "who I am in Christ."
Meaning in life and feelings of success	Based on how God sees the person and his relationship with Him.	Based on my actions and others' response to me	Centered in God, His will, and His pleasure in me.
Focus of Life	God and His will.	Self: "My interests, desires, wants, own world, good life."	God and His will. Self seen as it relates to God.
Method of Responding to Pressure and Problems	Left in God's hands. Able to handle it well.	Handled by self; often unbearable stress.	God given all cares and pressures, calm in life's storms.
Closeness to God	Intimate relationship; probably face to face.	Varying levels	Intimate relationship.

1. **Financial Security.** In this fast-paced environment, many are afraid of making a lifestyle change because it might include a drop in income. Most of us are simply too dependent upon our current income to adapt to a lifestyle that would make us happier. Debt is all too common and we cannot afford to relocate.

The nineties began with a depressed economy, a crisis in job markets and a fear that health insurance might not be available. Not surprisingly, many of us opt for security: *How can I walk away from a sure thing? I'm in a successful career now. Why risk a change?*

2. Family Matters. Moving to a new area or changing your lifestyle generates fears for the welfare of your family. A change in income may represent a change in schools, church, social life, and friends.

Parents are fearful that there will not be a better life in the future for their children. "In 2000 most new jobs will require schooling beyond high school. This will drive up unemployment rates among less educated workers. The cycle of poverty will become even more vicious as low income parents find themselves unable to send their children to college. If there is no attempt to stop current trends, half of all children born in New York City this year will face the same problems."[3]

3. Confused Priorities. Most of us are not able to balance our time between job, family, friends, and personal needs. We find we are unable to decide what's important in life. We are unclear about those missing elements that would make life complete and give us a feeling of "wholeness."

We strain to keep it together, but the internal and external pressures are so great we feel like we are caught in a vise with an ever tightening grip. For many it is like being on a fast-spinning merry-go-round. In trying to get off we are afraid we may lose our balance, fall, and get hurt. Why take the chance? Yet at the same time, we know that if we don't get off, we'll never get where we want to go. We'll just keep going around in dizzying circles.

We are caught in the dilemma of confused priorities. We can't find the answers to such questions as

- What is my purpose for living?
- What's missing to provide meaning in life?
- How do I satisfy my need for significance?
- Why are my relationships falling apart?
- How did I get so far in debt?
- What am I chasing? How did I get caught in this Rat Race?

When confusion exists in these basic elements of life, it will naturally spill over into all areas of our existence. We want the good life so desperately, but our culture has its own ideas about how to attain this good life, ideas far different than God's standards.

4. Fear. Change often means taking a chance, taking risks. We are afraid of not knowing exactly what will happen if we step off the fast track. Our security naturally diminishes when we recognize that we must do something about our lives. Fear is a natural part of this. Experience has shown me one thing—every new situation has its problems. No wonder we question the wisdom of making such a change: *If I step off this fast track with all its known problems, will I be getting myself into a worse set of problems?*

One of the greatest fears we all experience is that of loneliness. The *Wall Street Journal,* May 25, 1993, reports:

> Baby Boomers will be better off in retirement than their parents were, but will probably be lonelier. . . . The proportion who won't have married by age 65 is projected to be 50% larger than it was for their parents. High divorce rates make it far less likely that the retired boomers will be living with spouses. . . . They estimate that more than one-third of the men and women born from 1946 to 1955 will be living alone when they enter retirement, compared with just over 20% in their parent's generation.[4]

5. Information Overload. We are bombarded with so much information that we get confused and end up unfocused. We find making decisions, even small ones, to be a major undertaking. Older people are especially susceptible to this problem. They like the familiar and are less adventuresome; they are more desirous of the known than the unknown.

Television is notorious for its role in this overload. The ads give their Best Sales pitches: Buy car "A"—it is really cool; car "B" is the best according to one survey; but on the other hand car "C" has the endorsement of Road and Track magazine; Consumers Guide thinks car "D" outperforms all others; nine out of ten owners of car "E" would buy it again; your favorite football player is advertising car "F"; and so it goes through ten more cars. The confusion can be almost paralyzing.

Even children are not immune from the pressures of the Rat Race. Just watch them in the grocery store as they try to choose one cereal from among the many dozen advertised on the programs they watch. Yes, sadly we have allowed our society to let our children get a taste of the Rat Race!

In the end, we have such an overload of information that we too often are unable to prioritize all the information or filter out the unimportant. When this happens, we start procrastinating because we either don't know what to do or we still need more time to get all the information. We can become restless, dissatisfied, pressured, and even incapable of acting. Pity the poor perfectionist in this kind of scenario! Only the most organized of us can wade through the volumes of information, process them and come out on the other side with a right conclusion.

The potential for such situations, along with other questions and fears, can run through our minds and keep us ineffective or side tracked. We need to recognize that the Enemy wants us to stay in the Rat Race. He wants us to be hampered, frustrated, and less than all that God created us to be. For this reason, he will do everything he can to cause questions, doubts, uncertainty, and especially, lack of full trust in God. He will create situations in society that will seem to demand a different set of rules for living today than the one we lived by in the past. The more confusion he can create in our minds while undermining our confidence in the Lord, the less chance there is that we will turn to the Lord for our solution. Our natural tendency will be to try to make it on our own.

Part of the solution is going to come from a strong faith in God. The more we get to know Him, the better we can trust Him to be able to meet our needs and to do all that He promises to do in His Word.

To begin to expose the lies we have been believing about ourselves, our situations, and our society, we must recognize how we got where we are in our society today. We have believed certain myths because our standards have changed as have priorities.

WHO SETS THE STANDARD?

We have been chasing the "American Dream" for generations. Each generation has expected that theirs would be better off than the one before. And since the 1920s, this seems to have been the case for the most part. But the nineties have awakened people to a whole new set of realities. The standard of living is not getting better. But what does that mean? What are the ramifications?

Patrick Morley believes that life used to be somewhat linear and consistent:[5]

Morley contends that the standard of living by which we gauge the success of each generation must be measured in more than one dimension. We must examine both the material and the moral, which would include values, relationships and spirituality. While the nineties has bred the "driven generation," we are just beginning to pick up the pieces from the shattered

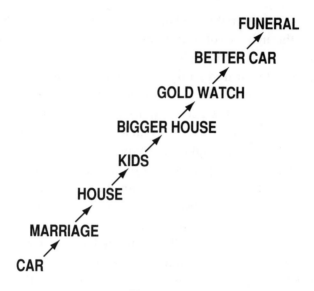

Figure 1-1

dreams and broken homes of the seventies and eighties. The problem lies in the fact that in the midst of unprecedented economic growth and material success, we have seen the degradation of society's morals.

Committed Christians see the end of the eighties and the first half of the nineties as a moral snowball which has picked up so much speed that many fear we are in an avalanche of moral degeneration, driven by political and media concerns, that will destroy all of our society. Criminal activity is out of control: increased suicide rates, failing educational standards, rampant disease, the disintegration of the family unit, and the devaluation of and media encouraged fear of Christians and their value system. All these are sweeping away what used to be one nation "under God." Today, there are no generally accepted moral standards in the United States; therefore, there is no solid, universal foundation from which lives are molded.

For the Christian, these standards should come from God's plumb line. Although society has changed its moral standards, God has not. Indeed, for many, this does present a dilemma. How do we measure our "success"? How do we determine our priorities? If we're not using God's standard, we'll be in trouble. In fact, there are seven warning signs that indicate a person may be trapped. Chapter 2 helps you identify these signs and gives you various tests to see whether or not you are caught in the Rat Race.

Chapter Two

Seven Warning Signs of Life in the Rat Race

Arnold Palmer, the famous golf champion, said that over the years he had watched hundreds of golfers. He had observed them as they meticulously practiced putting, and he had watched them practice their swings down the fairway. But in all his times on the practice tee, he had never once seen a golfer practicing how to get out of a sand trap.

Golfers rightly fear the hazards of sand traps, yet few can avoid them completely. At some time our course in life will catch us in a "sand trap." The danger is that we may be unprepared to deal with the tough situations in life.

Jesus said, "In this world you will have trouble. But take heart! I have overcome the world" (John 16:33). The problem with our lifestyle, however, is that we get so busy with the *bitter* now and now, that we forget that there will be a sweet by and by.

I have always had the ability to do more than one thing at a time. I often see myself as the comedian I grew up watching on the Ed Sullivan Show who would get one plate spinning on a stick. Then once it had begun spinning, he would get another plate spinning, and so on. He would continue his stunt until he would have about twenty different plates spinning. All the while, he was running back and forth trying to give each plate just enough momentum not to fall to the ground and break. That's too often been me!

Everyday during my morning shower and on my brief drive to work, I am already preparing in my mind which plates I will be spinning for the day. Of course, I would not go anywhere without my Franklin Planner, probably the most significant tool in my life apart from my Bible. I have left it at a restaurant or in the office only to find myself lost and wasting the next several hours backtracking because I didn't want to miss an appointment, let somebody down, hurt somebody's feelings, or appear unproductive.

I'm the kind of person who works better without a break. When interrupted, I lose momentum. I'll spend four hours working on one project, eat lunch on the run or make it a working lunch at a restaurant, and immediately get back to the project. I want to get it finished. I have a compulsion to accomplish. My wife worries about my driving to teach at Biola University. I listen to tapes *and* take notes, read a book, or even practice a talk, all at 55 mph (plus or minus).

I usually have work with me. I guess I'm afraid of being bored. In fact I'm writing this while watching two separate channels on the television in our living room. Have I gotten into the Rat Race? I don't like to think so when I love my work so, but . . . !

Is productivity the key to happiness? What will be the reward of doing a good job, of being a good guy, of following all the rules? Maybe it's a sense of accomplishment. Maybe it's just more of the Rat Race.

In the midst of this helter skelter, I have recognized seven signs of life in the fast track. People make the mistake of trying to medicate their fears and emotional hurts by maintaining a pace that removes them from reality. These external signs are sometimes hard to spot while you're spinning your plates. They appear so good on the outside; how could there be anything wrong with them? What we must do is look underneath the veneer and recognize those things that throw our lives out of balance. Then we must seek God's strategy to nurture what is missing on the inside.

WARNING SIGN #1 — BROWNOUTS

I once lived in a city in the high desert where the draw on the electricity would be so great in the summer that periodic brownouts would occur. The lights did not go out. My digital clocks didn't start blinking. Nonetheless, you could sense a difference. The lights grew dimmer.

People in the Rat Race have these same symptoms. There is such a draw on their thoughts and attention that they seem to forget recent conversations and events, not because of memory loss, but because of preoccupation or overload.

Here's a little quiz to see if you are prone to brownouts. Answer yes or no to the following questions.

YES NO

❑ ❑ 1. I wake up with headaches in the morning and begin my day with aspirin at least two days per week.

❑ ❑ 2. I find I'm easily discouraged and feel like crying over the silliest things.

❑ ❑ 3. I'm always tired. I don't feel creative and have trouble concentrating.

❑ ❑ 4. I don't get as much done as I used to. I feel mentally exhausted.

❑ ❑ 5. I just want to be alone. I don't look forward to coming home.

❑ ❑ 6. I have no hobbies; I don't have the patience or the energy.

❑ ❑ 7. I get mad too often. I lash out at my friends and family.

❑ ❑ 8. I appear to have a lower sex drive today than a month ago.

❑ ❑ 9. I get that "uptight" feeling in my stomach at least once a week. Antacids usually solve the problem.

❑ ❑ 10. I could use a neck or shoulder rub every day to help me get to sleep at night.

❑ ❑ 11. I've been making some bad decisions lately. My friends tell me I need a vacation.

❑ ❑ 12. I just can't sit still. And when I do, I feel guilty because I have so much to do.

To score this tool, simply add up the number of your "yes" answers.

0 – 3   Brownout? What's a brownout?

4 – 6   I possibly have a brownout once or twice a year.

7 – 9   I'm prone to brownouts; I struggle with my schedule.

10 – 12 Brown is my color! I'm a card-carrying member of the Rat Race!

The final eight chapters of this book are designed for those of you with high scores and will help those of you with lower scores better understand those who score high on this test.

The mind influences whether or not we have brownouts. It can either help us avoid pressures or cause us much more pressure, which can result in an inability to handle such pressures. If people are always complaining to themselves about all they have to do, if they allow themselves to feel pressured because they have failed to plan, if they look too much at circumstances and not at their Lord who has promised to meet all their needs, then indeed they will have a constant and real struggle to survive the Rat Race. Their mind may want to flee the pressure, and brownouts will result.

Part of this brownout will often be a negative and depressed attitude. On many occasions, Jesus had every reason to look at His situation and the responses of those around Him and say, "Forget it! This is too hard. All they do is grumble and gripe. They are never satisfied. These people will never learn. Why should I waste my time with them? This is a no-win situation. They will be the death of me if I don't watch out!" But we don't read anything even close to this. We do read about a heart of compassion: "O Jerusalem, Jerusalem . . . how often I have longed to gather your children together, as a hen gathers her chicks under her wings, but you were not willing." We do see a servant, washing the very feet of the ones who were His disciples, who would soon all desert Him, one of whom would go so far as to deny he ever knew Him. In fact Jesus even washed the feet of and later gave a kiss of friendship to the one He knew was betraying Him and sending Him to the cross.

How did Jesus keep a positive attitude in such circumstances? He kept His focus on His goals and did not look at the circumstances—only the goal. He knew where He was going and what the outcome would be. This is why we read about Jesus, "For the joy that was set before Him [He] endured the cross" (Heb. 12:2, KJV).

Jesus is our example. He blazed the trail. This is why no trap can capture those who keep their thoughts under the control of Jesus Christ as He asked us to do in 2 Corinthians 10:5. Choosing to look to the Lord for His provision, avoiding negative self-talk, repeating Scripture, and praying can all be instrumental in avoiding the negative, depression-causing factors of the Rat Race.

We've looked at what happens when we try to squeeze too much into our lives: We hurry. Now let's see how we can emotionally react when things don't go our way and the pressure is building.

WARNING SIGN #2 — NO FUN ALLOWED

The Rat Race is no place to slow down, relax, and have fun. There is always one more task to accomplish, one more job to do, one more committee to guide, and one more compulsion to fulfill. People caught in this lifestyle see fun as being counterproductive. They believe that no one gets anywhere in life by relaxing. Fun is at the bottom of the priorities because it demonstrates one's inability to enjoy work and excel. People who are caught in the Rat Race inevitably get very tired, but they have so fooled themselves that they see exhaustion as a badge of honor: *Look how hard I'm working. What a good person I am to sacrifice this way for those I love.* And their self-esteem gets massaged along with their tired feet, and their aching back and neck.

This warning sign leaves little space for reading, for fun, inspirational reading, physical exercise, prayer, hobbies, or anything else which hints at veering away from the day's priorities. Consider the following statements. The more "yes" answers you get to the following twelve questions, the less healthy fun you are allowing yourself to have.

YES NO

❏ ❏ 1. No one gets anywhere in life by relaxing.

❏ ❏ 2. Even when I have time, I'm too tired to do anything fun or relaxing.

❏ ❏ 3. My state of exhaustion makes me feel that I am worthwhile.

❏ ❏ 4. My work is more important than my own personal comfort or desires.

❏ ❏ 5. When I rest, I feel guilty.

☐ ☐ 6. I never feel that I accomplish enough, even though I am exhausted all the time from the long hours I put in.

☐ ☐ 7. I don't think that taking time off to have fun would relieve my stress.

☐ ☐ 8. Laughter should not be part of the workplace.

☐ ☐ 9. A lunch break is for eating and not for entertainment.

☐ ☐ 10. I often have work with me when I eat a meal.

☐ ☐ 11. I take a "To Do" list with me on vacations.

☐ ☐ 12. I choose to attend a business meeting rather than my child's school function.

WARNING SIGN #3 — IMPATIENCE

People caught in the Rat Race always feel that they are behind, so they become impatient easily. They overcommit, overcompensate, and overindulge. A friend on the East Coast put it this way: "The faster I get to the office, the more I can get done. The more I get done, the more time I will have to devote to catching up on those things I'm behind on. The more I catch up, the more I want out."

Time is now the hottest commodity in our economy. The Rat Race dictates people and their schedules. We don't like to be kept waiting. Nor do we like lines. We get upset if something is not in stock and has to be ordered. Let's face it, we are impatient. And impatience leads to hurrying, and a hurried lifestyle generates stress. Our impatience causes us to live on the ragged edge. The impatient, hurried person sets unrealistic deadlines and attempts to find as many short cuts as possible. All too frequently these people sacrifice a quality home life or relationship to feed the adrenaline flow of living life in the fast lane. The more they do, the better they feel.

But they set themselves up for great stress when they fail to live life with reserves. By living life with reserves, I mean arriving a little early so you will not have to hurry, or paying your bills early so you will not have to worry about late notices. It means getting your paper written early, so that when the deadline approaches, you don't have to collapse from exhaustion after an "all-nighter" to get it done.

People in the Rat Race become grumpy and irritable, even angry when things do not go as planned. This can lead to poor decision-making as they attempt to bypass the delay. They may launch a project with only half the data compiled or half the options evaluated. Gathering data and testing alternatives take time and patience, but in the Rat Race there often is no time to do so.

So here's your test to see how impatient you are.

YES NO

❑ ❑ 1. If a TV show ends with "To be continued," I feel frustrated and let down because I don't want to wait.

❑ ❑ 2. I could never live in an area that has a large amount of traffic jams.

❑ ❑ 3. When a friend is telling me a story that seems to drag on, I find myself looking at my watch.

❑ ❑ 4. Places like check out lines and the Post Office wreak havoc with my stress levels.

❑ ❑ 5. Reading my Bible seems to take away time from the important things I have to do.

❑ ❑ 6. Driving the speed limit is no longer an option because I'm always a little behind.

❑ ❑ 7. If I do not sense where a book is going in the first few chapters, I will most likely put it down or read the final chapter to see the ending.

❑ ❑ 8. I don't like planting seeds in my garden because by nature I want to dig them up and see how they're doing.

❑ ❑ 9. I have a tendency to finish sentences for other people.

❑ ❑ 10. I love to watch God change people but tend to nag at them to change quickly.

❑ ❑ 11. I change lanes frequently on the freeway because the other lane always moves faster.

❑ ❑ 12. I'd rather make a phone call than write a letter because I can get the answer more quickly.

WARNING SIGN #4 — PERFECTIONISM

My wife has perfectionist tendencies and often feels like a card-carrying member of the Rat Race. Perfectionists are ruthless in self-evaluation. Their inner drive can be depressing for both themselves and others as they continually push to set and achieve higher standards.

At the very core of this warning sign is an innate fear of failure and rejection. Adam and Eve showed this tendency. There they were, created by God to be at peace in a garden of peace. One wrong choice and sin entered the world. What was their first response? "We'd better hide. God's not going to be happy with what we've done. He gave us the Garden, told us to take care of it and we blew it." They were afraid of rejection due to their moral failure.

Fear causes us to become critical. *What if I don't get the promotion? I can't get a "B" on the test; I must get an "A." I sure hope I can meet the church's standards; I really want to be a leader. The house had better be clean or Mom's going to let us know.* There is no pleasing the perfectionist. The main problem for the perfectionist is the inability to distinguish between the "I should's" and the "I could's." Overuse of the words "should" or "ought" drive into you the inability to meet your own standards. Your self-esteem then plummets.

Changing your terminology takes away much of the finger pointing and blame. Saying "could" introduces the element of choice. I *could* have washed the car today, but I chose not to. I *could* have worked overtime today, but I chose not to.

Here are twelve statements to help you see how much of a perfectionist you are.

YES NO

☐ ☐ 1. I can't sit through even a half hour TV show without getting up to do something during the commercials.

☐ ☐ 2. I have to look at many selections before buying the "right" gift.

☐ ☐ 3. When I listen to a sermon, I easily pick up on grammatical mistakes.

☐ ☐ 4. I can't stand a messy desk or work space.

☐ ☐ 5. I often find it takes a long time to finish a project because I keep thinking of new ways to improve it.

☐ ☐ 6. I am always straightening up after family members, even when they are not finished with the item.

☐ ☐ 7. I can often think of a better way to do something than the way someone else did it.

☐ ☐ 8. It takes me a long time to decide what to wear to special occasions.

❏ ❏ 9. I walk into a room and notice if a picture on the wall is crooked.

❏ ❏ 10. When I got a "B" on a test, I felt my world was crashing in on me.

❏ ❏ 11. I never start anything I know I can't do well.

❏ ❏ 12. It drives me up a wall to see the greeting cards out of place in the store, so I straighten them.

WARNING SIGN #5 — LOSING YOUR FIRST LOVE

Remember how great those first days, weeks, even years were with the Lord? The times with Him in Bible reading and prayer were so special. What ever happened to them? The Rat Race—that's what happened. We've gotten caught up in the hurry, the pressures, and stress of life. Relationships, as we will soon see, have gotten strained, and our excitement about the Lord has drained out as the pressures and concerns have flowed in. The urgent has become a tyrant and our priorities have gotten confused. Our once strong desire to be with the Lord and enjoyment with Him have become dulled, uninteresting, and at times, (we are embarrassed to admit) almost a burden. Why? Because we have allowed our love for Him to be "choked by life's worries, riches and pleasures . . . " (Luke 8:14).

The following quiz will help you see how far you have gone down the road away from your First Love.

YES NO

❏ ❏ 1. I used to have a lot of joy and excitement in my Christian life. Now it seems so dull, so routine.

❏ ❏ 2. Praying used to be easy for me, but now I find I struggle in it.

❏ ❏ 3. It seems like I miss my quiet times much easier these days than when I was first born again.

❏ ❏ 4. When I read the Bible, I don't get much out of it. That has not always been the case.

❏ ❏ 5. Sometimes I find myself questioning God's love and care for me.

❏ ❏ 6. It has been some time since I've shared my faith with anyone.

❑ ❑ 7. I rarely will mention my faith at work.

❑ ❑ 8. Most people probably don't know I am a born again Christian.

❑ ❑ 9. Sometimes I wonder if God really has a good plan for my life.

❑ ❑ 10. I have some bitterness, resentment, or anger towards God.

❑ ❑ 11. I don't seem to have much motivation to go to church these days.

❑ ❑ 12. Even though I know it is the right thing to do, I don't find it easy to get very involved in church activities.

WARNING SIGN #6 — STRAINED RELATIONSHIPS

Some people handle their personal pain by isolating themselves. Others on the fast track use their personal pace as a sedative. They keep so busy that they have no time for other people nor to think about their own perceived inadequacies or past failures. They hope that what they accomplish today will offset any weaknesses or past problems.

This happens many times in the ministry. Caring for others can be overwhelming. The minister becomes a "churchaholic." The spouse and family take a back seat to programs. Because only so much energy and so many thoughts are available, the minister who keeps them focused on his work will not have time for much else. The result is strained relationships.

Although accomplished in their field, people who fail to heed this warning sign find that the people around them are neglected and anticipating "second best." Don't get me wrong, this concept is not gender relative. Husbands and wives both can become "wedded to work." Men and women can become too busy for their partners and friends. Socializing takes a back seat to the tension to get ahead or just caught up.

Eventually, the dreaded bargaining takes place. "Honey, you get me out of this party, and we'll have more time together next week." "Sugar, just let me spend one of our two weeks of vacation working on this project, and I'll make it up to you." Will they ever cut back? Not in the Rat Race. It is a hard taskmaster and a jealous mistress.

So, how strained are your relationships?

YES   NO

❑   ❑   1. I leave a trail of hurt feelings even though the job gets done.

❑   ❑   2. People ignore me because I don't seem to have enough time for them.

❑   ❑   3. I get into arguments over the silliest details.

❑   ❑   4. I often open my mouth just long enough to exchange feet.

❑   ❑   5. In any given week, I sense tension between myself and at least one other person.

❑   ❑   6. I tend to be intolerant with my children, not allowing them to make mistakes.

❑   ❑   7. I sometimes say things that I later wish I could take back.

❑   ❑   8. At times I feel like I'm "walking on egg shells" with certain people.

❑   ❑   9. It is more important for me to be right than to consider another person's point of view.

❑   ❑   10. When I sense a conflict with someone, I will rarely return his or her phone call.

❑   ❑   11. I don't compromise very well.

❑   ❑   12. I get my feelings hurt easily.

WARNING SIGN #7 — MISAPPROPRIATED PRIORITIES

Psychologists have a term to describe people who are caught up in the Rat Race. The term is *obsessive-compulsive*. Such people may think they are doing all right in life because they get so much accomplished. But in reality they may be stressed out, critical, and driven by all the things they "ought" to do. They aren't satisfied with their own performance or that of others. Rarely can they accomplish enough. They always push themselves to their limits or beyond, leaving no cushion of time for emergencies or for something that is of a higher priority. The resulting frustration and emotional strain often cause them to crash and take others with them on the way down.

This mindset leaves them with unfinished projects—partially read books, half-completed tasks—that have gotten set aside. Something else came up that seemed a higher priority. They give up on their goal because they hit a snag and do not want to take the time to find a solution. They feel the constant self-imposed pressure with projects or with people. If a project is not coming together right, it is easier to abandon the whole thing than to have something hanging around that is causing them problems. A critical spirit and also guilt can easily flow out of such a scenario. Time becomes a factor blown out of proportion, and people can get bruised by the fallout of such a lifestyle. Take the following quiz to see how your priorities stand.

YES NO

☐ ☐ 1. Sometimes little things bother me so much I can't concentrate on more important things.

☐ ☐ 2. I only read my Bible in times of crisis.

☐ ☐ 3. I don't think prayer has as much power as people say it does.

☐ ☐ 4. My first priority is earning a living for my family.

☐ ☐ 5. Church is a good place for my children to get involved, but not for me.

☐ ☐ 6. I have no need to tell the people closest to me that I love and appreciate them because they already know it.

☐ ☐ 7. I haven't sat down with my children this month to tell them how special they are to me.

☐ ☐ 8. There has been a person who has touched me deeply in the last year, to whom I failed to write a note of encouragement.

☐ ☐ 9. I will probably have regrets on my deathbed that I didn't spend more time with my family.

☐ ☐ 10. I have left a trail of unfinished projects over the last year.

☐ ☐ 11. I start an exercise or a diet but soon lose interest.

☐ ☐ 12. I don't need to tune up my car today; the car's running just fine.

BALANCE IS THE KEY

How do we get in such a state? It is usually in one of two ways. Either we have the right priorities but have allowed them to get out of balance, or we have wrong priorities that have been self-determined and not God determined.

God created us with the need for balance in all things. We see it everywhere. We know the earth must be in balance so it will not spin off into space. We need a balanced diet or we can get sick—high cholesterol, weak bones, skin problems, and heart disease. The architect knows well the need for balance in design. If he makes a big enough mistake, disaster can result.

We see this same principle in all areas of our lives. Work is a good thing. I love my responsibilities as a pastor. Speaking for Promise Keepers and various other conferences is a good thing. My family is wonderful. Writing books is good. Coaching Little League sports is fun. All these things and so many more that make up my life are good. But if I let any one area of a good thing take too much time, it cannot help but create a detrimental imbalance in my life.

I have learned that there are certain foundational things on which I cannot compromise: personal time with the Lord, enough time with each family member, sermon preparation, time with my staff, proper diet and adequate rest. The next level is of important things that should be done and that I want to do, which are allowed to take a chunk of the remaining time: counseling, certain writing, various speaking opportunities, coaching, and spending time with friends. Finally, there are the remaining items, which if I can get to them, will please me, but I can live without them: repairing an old car, doing extra things with the family, more study, writing and speaking, even more rest and recreation—a list that is long but not very reasonable by themselves. I realize that I must prioritize my activities if I am to avoid imbalance and the resulting consequences, including the guilt, short temper, pressure, and frustration that come from being out of balance.

Many people have allowed good qualities to be pushed too far, thus bringing them into an imbalance that creates wrong priorities. Our homes offer a prime example.

Keeping the Home Fires Burning

Consider the dilemma of the man who loves his family so much that he spends all his time earning money to give them the best life. But in the end he loses his family because he spends such long hours working and is never there for his family when they have special occasions or while they are simply growing up. Recently a man came to me, an executive in a Los Angeles area space company. He sat in the chair, weeping, shaking, and almost incoherent as he poured out his story. "Everything I've worked for is gone. My wife has kicked me out and is taking the kids, saying I'm never home so why should I keep my things there? What am I going to do? They are my whole reason for working!" When we have a life out of balance, with wrong priorities even for right reasons, the results can be devastating.

A classic song by Harry Chapin, "The Cat's in the Cradle," describes just such a situation. The father is always just about to be there for his son, but never quite makes it. At various stages of his childhood and teenage years the son asks, "When you coming home, Dad?" Each time the father replies, "I don't know when. But we'll get together then." Misplaced priorities. And the song shows it. For when the father is finally ready and eager to spend time with his son, the son has learned from his father how not to be there for his father. Thus, when the father asks his adult son, "When you coming home, son?" his son replies, "I don't know when. But we'll get together then."

Unfortunately, this tragedy happens with mothers, too. They get so busy with careers, social or church activities, or being caught up in making the home perfect that they have no quality time with the children or their husband. Eventually, the family will suffer. This may cause the mother to feel guilty, which just adds more pressure. The solution is to evaluate present priorities by deciding how much really has to be done. Does the house have to be dusted every day? Is it important to have every little thing in place? How perfect does the child's room need to be in order not to inhibit the child's expression of his own personality? (Loosening this one priority might relieve a lot of tension in a family.)

Teamwork is a key to balance in the home. Kids can help with chores. A husband who sees his working wife overwhelmed with household duties or who wants her to keep the home kept perfect needs to pitch in and help her.

Finding a Spiritual Focus

Prayer is an important part of any person's life. The busy person will often find that this important element is being squeezed out by all the activities he or she is involved in. Apart from the vital necessity of having a special time alone with the Lord, a person can add extra time to this while driving, doing chores, or getting ready for work. Even the shower can provide a time to talk with the Lord about things on your heart or to express your love and appreciation for Him. Keeping handy a card with a Scripture verse on it can be a nice way of memorizing Scripture while you're doing a routine task.

Today's generation has been conditioned to be entertained from sunup to sundown. Television, movies, games, recreational activities—all these and much more have shaped a mentality that craves input and variety. One way to take advantage of this mentality and to keep a spiritual focus in the middle of the pressures of the Rat Race is to have praise songs, Christian radio, or Bible tapes playing while doing housework or driving, even while dressing or getting ready to go out. This helps keep boredom at bay, makes the work go faster, and nourishes the soul and spirit.

We need God's wisdom to avoid misplaced priorities. He is eager to give it. Ask Him how to have balance and then put into place what He shows you.

WRONG PRIORITIES

At times there may seem to be a fine line between misplaced priorities and the second cause for problems, wrong priorities. The first was a good thing that became bad because it was out of balance. The second is wrong because it never was right to begin with. These priorities are self determined and not God determined. Too often a person will decide what he wants and then ask God to bless his choice. The right way is to ask God what His priorities are, and then follow them. This means giving up our self-centered ways and having real trust in the Lord.

People caught in this performance trap are usually driven because they are works-oriented. They have been conditioned by family and friends to believe that their value comes not from who they are but from what they do. As a result, they must always be performing. They can even transfer this obsession and impose it as a standard on other people, too, when they are in the position of being the model for someone such as a child or a subordinate.

Often the person who is caught up in the Rat Race is only focusing on what is in front of him at the moment. He is willing to sacrifice everything, including health, happiness, and others in order to reach his goals. He takes no time for anything that will pull him away from his goals or sidetrack him for something else that may seem to interfere. And yet, the paradox is that he often will say yes to something that seems appealing even though he is already overcommitted.

Joshua is just such a person. He works hard at his insurance business, spends evenings with clients, and spends weekends contacting those he missed during the week. But he also loves sports. So do his children. His oldest son plays tailback at the high school. Another son is in track, and his daughter plays volleyball. When he can, Joshua loves to participate in a good game of football or baseball. Last year, he coached a Little League team which had an impressive season. It was hard to squeeze in the time to do the coaching, but he sacrificed to do so. What he often sacrificed was the privilege of seeing his own kids' sporting events. This caused some guilt, but the thrill of competition and the excitement of the moment were stronger pulls than the resulting guilt. When he was asked to coach a swimming team, he hesitated for a moment, but its special place in his heart won out so he added that to his already packed schedule. Family members cringed when they heard that Dad had another thing to do, since they already saw so little of him. But they knew he worked long, hard hours. They did not want their own disappointment to take away things from him that seemed so important to him. So they hid their feelings because they concluded that they should not expect him to be more involved in their lives than he presently was.

LET GOD GIVE BALANCE

I can almost hear some of you saying, "Glen's describing me! But how do I get the right priorities?" It is not easy, because it takes a big step of faith. But it is necessary if you are ever to have victory over the Rat Race. The first step is to turn your whole life and all you are involved in back to God, asking Him what He wants you to be doing. Where should you be working, what new responsibilities should you take on? What do you need to give up? These last two points are important, because probably part of your lifestyle includes taking on almost every job you are asked to do because you so want to please others and be acceptable to them. Often you quickly say yes, only to regret it almost before the word is out of your mouth.

This brings us to the second step: When a new opportunity presents itself, allow God to set your priorities and show you what you can and cannot do at any given time. Statements like "Let me pray about that" (if you really intend to, of course) or "I'll get back to you" will help you give yourself time to evaluate before the Lord what you should be doing.

The final step is to let God help you set your priorities from this moment forward so that they will be the right ones. Our priorities determine what our actions will be. Part of setting priorities is not to look to self or circumstances, but to God. God says that when we have our eyes on Him, He will guide us. In fact, God did not choose just to tell us how to avoid problems, He gave us a beautiful example in the person of Jesus Christ, who was able to live successfully in a world full of pressures, rejections, misunderstandings, and evil—a world that would eventually kill Him. Did He get caught in the Rat Race? Indeed, He did not! As we examine His life, we will see ways in which He modeled for us how to avoid the traps of the Rat Race. Throughout the rest of the book, we will see how Jesus modeled for us what we need to do.

So What's the Answer?

The seven warning signs that I have identified in this chapter each need to be evaluated and addressed individually. Chapters 6 through 12 suggest ways to overcome the warning signs. Despite the fact that there will be some overlap in each of these areas, I have tried to present the major reason each one is a factor in the Rat Race.

Brownout, the first warning sign, is answered in chapter 6. When we reach a point where we are forgetful and not functional, it is time to learn our limits. Jesus knew the right time for everything. He did not try to do all of His ministry at once, but instead spaced it out over three-and-a-half years.

You remember that having no fun was the second warning sign, and we will see in chapter 7 that there is a desperate need for wise decision making when trapped in this mindset. Unwise decisions that they have made caused people to feel pressured and boxed in and may keep them from feeling that they can take any time for themselves.

The third warning sign, impatience, will be discussed in chapter 8 as we break the cycle of busyness and learn how to manage our time correctly. Jesus met with the Father daily to plan what He was to do. He told his disciples that he did nothing apart from what the Father showed Him. He had a plan and followed it.

Perfectionism, the fourth warning sign, is detailed in chapter 9 in which we will learn how to make allowances for others as we put aside perfectionism. You might remember that Jesus was extremely patient with His disciples who never seemed to grasp all the lessons that He was presenting to them. Yet, He rarely scolded them saying, "now shape up and get with the program or I'll find other disciples." Surely His patience must have been a key part of the disciples' love for Him.

Losing your first love is the fifth warning sign and finds its answer in chapter 10, "Return to Your First Love." Find out how to strengthen your walk with God.

The sixth sign, strained relationships, is often caused by self-centeredness. Demanding your rights and seeking your personal wants and desires tends to generate an ingrown outlook. Building community will forge strong, lasting relationships. Jesus had ample opportunity to have strained relationships. One of his closest friends was a thief who eventually betrayed Him. Yet Jesus treated him with great love and care. Even when Peter betrayed Him, He did not act hurt or have a pity-party. Instead Jesus forgave him and helped Peter get back on track and feel accepted again. Chapter 11 will help you do the same.

Chapter 12 will address the way to correct warning sign number seven, misappropriated priorities. We get in trouble when we fail to follow God's plan for our lives, by doing what we feel is best instead. Establishing a life map according to God's will for your life will go a long way in helping you sense fulfillment and direction. Jesus had such a map. Even at age twelve he knew that He must be about His Father's business (Luke 2:49). At the end of His earthly life Jesus could earnestly say, "It is finished" (John 19:29).

So, there you have it. Seven answers to seven pitfalls of the Rat Race's maze. Inevitably, all seven of these warning signs cause a person to drift away from God. The intent of this book is to draw you back, get your life back under control, and "order" your priorities.

It is now time to look at some more practical applications of running this race successfully, of real traps we need to avoid. A look at the elements of the good life will help us do just that.

PART TWO

Taking Stock

Chapter Three

What Is the Good Life?

My wife, Nancy, and I lived in a tiny, six-hundred-square-foot apartment when we were first married. Living in a poor part of town, but close to our university, our only aspiration was to break into the middle class, which we defined as having a two-bedroom apartment. Actually buying a home was beyond our wildest dreams. About four years later, we purchased our first home, a modest two-bedroom home in desperate need of some minor care like paint, repairs, and lots of yard work. But living in that home was a touch of heaven. We could make do with two or three hours of yard work each week and periodic sanding of the hardwood floors.

Or could we? After two-and-a-half years, we discovered we were no longer satisfied. The newness of home ownership had worn off. We found ourselves on the prowl, searching for a larger, newer, three-bedroom home.

Three homes later we are truly content, or are we? In the midst of our never-enough world, there is always plenty more to want, and I've made a startling realization—always wanting is symptomatic of life in the Rat Race.

UNDERSTANDING THE TIMES

Tired of hearing about materialism? Tired of being accused of it? In our never-satisfied culture, materialism is not only a way of life, it is part of the American Dream. Turn on your television, read a magazine, or talk with friends over dinner and you will see that life's greatest struggles can and will be answered by attaining and achieving. After all, "you deserve a break today" because "you're worth it."

We live in an environment which thrives on the "If only" syndrome. *If only I had a bigger paycheck, then I'd be happy. If only we owned a nicer home. . . . If only I had that car . . . If we live in the correct place, wear the right clothes, and enjoy vacations at the choicest spots, "We've arrived."*

Too many people struggle with "destination disease," desperately hoping that their lives and families will be better when they arrive. Most reach the middle of their life crying out, "Stop the world I want to get off!" or "Get me out of this Rat Race!" But they are afraid of "stopping their world"—fearful it will suddenly throw them into a worse situation. So they stay in their Rat Race and suffer, getting more and more frustrated as their life races out of control.

THOSE BABY BOOMERS AGAIN

The typical lifestyle of baby boomers, those born between 1946 and 1964, has not always been the norm. The pre-1946 generation, known as the "Builder" generation, characterized their lives with saving. They had survived the Depression and two world wars, and were determined not to be left "without" again. They saved everything, from cartons in which the eggs arrived to excess pieces of felt. After all, "You never know when you're going to need it."

Along came the baby boomers, the most studied generation in recent history. They neither needed nor lacked anything. Whereas the builders had saved, the boomers spent. Whereas the builders had been careful in their purchasing, the boomers were rather frivolous with their money. Landon Jones describes the era to which the boomers were introduced like this: "For most of human history, people had thought that life was hard, brutal, and tragic. But the baby boomer's early affluence developed in it . . . 'the psychology of entitlement.' What other generations have thought privileges, the baby boomers thought were rights."[2]

I read Jones' article and thought to myself, "He's right." We aren't satisfied with our current lifestyle unless it is seen as a stepping stone to something better. It doesn't matter that most of the world will never have the opportunity for the affluence that we enjoy. The average lifestyle in America would seem like that of a rich person's in any Third World country. It's all wrapped up in the attitude of getting more, owning more, more . . . more . . . More!

Getting to the Root of the Problem

I must confess, I am easily swayed by the tides of culture. What I have learned however, is that the source of current discontent runs far deeper oijy than cultural tendencies. When sin and rebellion toward God rear their ugly heads, the resulting emptiness cannot be filled by purchases or upgrades. No matter how much I own, I will never be able to fill the emptiness of my soul.

You've probably heard before, "Money cannot buy happiness." But, be honest, is it not a little unrealistic to say that you have never enjoyed having money and the things money can buy? I love my home in southern California. I love my income. I do not have any guilt for them because my hope is not fixed on them: "Instruct those who are rich in this present world not to be conceited or to fix their hope on the uncertainly of riches, but on God, who richly supplies us with all things to enjoy" (I Tim. 6:17, NASB).

What I am saying is that life is a matter of tradeoffs. If am chasing the almighty dollar, my family will suffer. If I travel too much for speaking, my wife's needs will be left unattended. A balanced perspective is the only answer because money, like all other worldly things, has its limitations. It can buy a house, but not a home. It can buy a bed, but not the peace of mind necessary for sleep. It can buy cleats, a glove, a soccer ball, and even a uniform, but not the availability of an interested father cheering for his children from the stands. Gifts and things are an expression of love, but in their very essence cannot *be* love.

Day after day, week after week, year often year, I must evaluate what is truly important in life in comparison to those fun things that will probably never completely satisfy. I don't care what that bumper sticker says, it is not the one who dies with the most toys that wins. It's the one who has loved God with all his heart, soul, and mind, and loved his neighbor as himself. These actions will take on the very tangible results of a godly family, a heart for others, and a desire to invest their lives in a purpose greater than themselves.

DANGERS OF MATERIALISM

Having said all this, we must all come to a point of evaluation. What do we expect out of life? How will we measure success? How much of ourselves will we give to the ones we really love? What is the real driving force behind this void, this emptiness that we are facing? As we consider the danger of measuring our success and happiness by the things we possess, we would do well to note the four ways that materialism will hurt us.

First, materialism generates worry. Matthew 6:25 reminds us, "Therefore, I tell you, do not worry about your life, what you will eat or drink; or about your body, what you will wear. Is not life more important than food, and the body more important than clothes?" Whatever you focus your attention and your time to, will generate worry. As a resident of earthquake plagued southern California, I can testify to the problem of owning delicate things like[3] good dishes. Many people have put their valuable breakable treasures away and will not see them again until they move out of the area, simply because the goods might get destroyed in a quake. How sad that they will never have the joy of using the expensive china and crystal on which they spent so much money.

But this is not the only type of worry generated by "things." Often luxury items or things that are more expensive and complicated than we really need can get us into trouble. The person who drives an ordinary vehicle probably does not get as upset about a scratch or a fender bender as the one who drives a Porsche or Lexus. Precious time that could be spent with family or friends is instead spent taking care of possessions

Second, materialism wears you out. Proverbs 23:4 speaks to this very issue by reminding us, "Do not wear yourself out to get rich; have the wisdom to show restraint." Haven't you noticed that when you are finally getting a little closer to "keeping up with your neighbors" that they refinance and you get further behind? Part and parcel to this Rat Race existence is the pace of life created by our inherent desire to attain. The very speed of it wears people down.

I am convinced that our desire to constantly get more is a ploy of Satan to create a desire that is satisfied by self and not by God, who alone is able to meet all our needs. This is why the Lord tell us to be content with what we have. He knows we can never be satisfied by things or the constant pursuit of possessions. Even trying to maintain all you own can be tiresome and frustrating. Is this not why many people pursue the "simple life?" They have come to the conclusion that what God has said is true (even if they do not recognize this is what they are affirming).

Third, materialism creates dissatisfaction. The more we get, the more we want; we can never be satisfied. In fact, God illustrates that in Psalm 106:15, in which He says that He grants the desires of the people's hearts, but brings leanness to their souls.

Have you ever seen a person who is satisfied with his or her wardrobe, even if it fills six closets? We are fascinated with stories about Imelda Marcos with her thousands of pairs of shoes or Jackie Kennedy with her ability to stretch even the pocket book of multimillionaires as she bought innumerable outfits. You never win at the game of attaining things. Materialism has such a negative effect on us. That is why God tells us we are to be content with what we have.

Fourth, materialism promotes depression. In 1 Timothy 6:10, Paul shares, "For the love of money is a root of all kinds of evil. Some people, eager for money, have wandered from the faith and pierced themselves with many griefs." When we find ourselves comparing our lifestyle, our income, and our accumulations with others, we get depressed. Television tells us, "you can have it all." That is not true. And when you have finally recognized this reality, depression can set in.

The Bible does not teach that it is wrong to be wealthy. Money is not the root of all evil, it is the "love of money" that is the root of all evil. Throughout the Bible, we find people who were extremely successful in their finances. Abraham and Job were probably among the wealthiest people of their time. We know Barnabas was a wealthy man because he was able to give money to the church. Joseph of Arimathea, who gave his family tomb to Jesus, was among the financially elite. The real issue is not the obtaining of money, but the misuse of it.

Our goal of the truly good life only comes when we put others before ourselves, saving before spending, and giving before receiving. This is one of the key principles that God reinforces throughout His Word in such passages as Ephesians 4:2–4, 29 which tells us to "Be completely humble and gentle; be patient, bearing with one another in love. Make every effort to keep the unity of the Spirit through the bond of peace" (NIV). Why? Because God knows that we are social beings and that we need to live in harmony with those around us. All the money in the world, all the possessions, all the good looks—nothing can give us peace in our hearts and true happiness if those around us are not in agreement with us.

FIVE STEPS TO THE GOOD LIFE

Finally, let's look at **five steps that will help insure that the good life that God intends for you will come to pass.**

1. Recognize that all you have comes originally from God. He gave you your skills, abilities, and good health so you could get a job. He even gave you the knowledge that the job existed and favor with the one doing the hiring. Therefore, consider yourself the guardian of all the monies He has entrusted to you. Also, do not be prideful in your accomplishments by drawing attention to how smart, how clever, or how talented you are. Walk in humility before the Lord, for the Lord resists the proud, we are told in James 4:6. By recognizing that what you have comes from God, you will also be able to trust Him with what He has given you to either keep it safe or to supply you with another in order to meet your needs as He has promised in Phillippians 4:19.

2. Pay your tithes. Then seek what the Lord wants you to do with any extra monies you have for offerings. We are given a wonderful promise in Malachi 3:10, "Bring the whole tithe into the storehouse, that there may be food in my house. Test me in this," says the Lord Almighty, "and see if I will not throw open the floodgates of heaven and pour out so much blessing that you will not have room enough for it." In verse eight God had just told the Jews that they were robbing Him of the tithes and offerings that were due Him. So God then lets them know what they are missing as a result of holding back from Him, the key source of the Good Life—His abundant blessings. Sadly, when it comes to giving, many suffer from an ailment called "cirrhosis of the giver." One writer describes it this way:

> "The disease cirrhosis of the giver was discovered in A.D. 34 by the husband-wife team of Ananias and Sapphira (Acts 5:1–11). It is an acute condition that renders the patient's hands immobile when he

is called on to move them in the direction of his wallet or her purse, and from thence to the offering plate. This strange malady is clinically unobservable in such surroundings as the golf club, supermarket, clothing store, or restaurant. Some try to use a fake remedy, pointing [out] to other patients that income tax deductions can be claimed for giving. The best therapy, and that which leads to a sure and lasting cure, is to get the individual's heart right with God. This affliction is actually a symptom of a more basic need of the soul."

You've heard these sayings before, "You can't take it with you." "You'll never see a hearse pulling a U-Haul behind it." "You came into this world with zero and you will leave the same way." So, "store up for yourselves treasures in heaven, where moth and rust do not destroy, and where thieves do not break in and steal. For where your treasure is, there your heart will be also" (Matt. 6:20–21). And how do you do that? By investing in those things that are going to be there: the people of God, God's Word, and God's work. I have always told our church that God does not need our money, but He does desire what our money represents, which is our hearts.

3. Ask the Lord to show you what you *really* need. Ask Him to help you separate your needs from your desires. We often let our desires get us into trouble by overextending ourselves; we buy things we really don't need and can't afford. A good question to ask ourselves is, "Is this really something I can't live without?" Another good series of question is, "Why am I buying this? Is it because I want it to keep up with others who are getting similar things? Is it because I want to feel better about myself and my status? Do I want others to notice me?" A valid reason to purchase something would be because it will help you be more efficient or in some other way make your quality of life better from a godly perspective. By sorting out your motives, you will be able better to evaluate how much you need the item. Remember, there are two other questions to ask yourself. "Can I afford this at this time? What else will suffer if I spend money for this item?" This process will help you determine your true needs.

4. Ask the Lord to change your wants if they are out of balance. Wants become out of balance when we have lost track of what is really important in life. We have started to focus on ourselves and on others more than on God. Ask Him to help you be content in whatever financial circumstance you may be in. You need His help to reprioritize your values and to be able to identify need versus greed. The fifth point will help you do this.

5. Make the Lord the source of your satisfaction. This is really the bottom line in defining the "good life." We need to choose not to focus on ourselves, but on the Lord. When we are so centered on the Lord and what He wants that other things cannot really steal away our joy, then we have positioned ourselves to be able to experience life as God means for us to.

Too often the Enemy has been able to take us down a detour, making us think happiness is just around the corner if only we will buy a certain thing. But if you are anything like me, you will have found over and over again that the "blue bird of happiness" flew the coop just before you bought this thing you could not live without. Truly, only the Lord can satisfy our souls. He alone can give us the significance, the meaning in life, and the satisfaction we try so hard to find in "things."

Once you have done the above five steps, you may find it very helpful to keep a record of *all* you spend, even the two cents for the gum machine, in order to get a handle on how and on what you are spending your money. Mark those things that are frivolous, spur-of-the-moment purchases. Then ask the Lord to help you cut down on such money zappers.

Some people find it helpful to make a shopping list and then buy only what is on the list. If you think you've found a real bargain, wait one or two days (if possible) but at least ten minutes to two-and-a-half hours before deciding to buy it. Pray about the purchase in the waiting time. Ask God to show you if you should buy it, and *listen* to Him. Then do what He shows even if you are disappointed because He has said no. One thing I do is to ask Him to also take away my desire for the item if He doesn't want me to have it. By the way, I usually know even before praying whether or not I truly need it.

SUMMARY

Taking these five steps will greatly help in reducing and avoiding many of the financial traps or pressures of the Rat Race. Christians know that God has promised them an abundant life. Yet many are far from experiencing it. That's one of the reasons why people ask, "If life's so good, why am I so unhappy?" We will explore that question in the next chapter.

Chapter Four

If Life's So Good, Why Am I So Unhappy?

It is not difficult to understand why so many people have bought into the modern version of success. Television, magazines, and billboards on every corner work to convince us that making money is the single road to success. But the media is only partially to blame. Religious convictions and traditions once that were thought to provide a semblance of peace and order to life have been replaced by short-order entertainment and a focus on self. "Deism" has been changed to "me-ism." Today's philosophies: "If it feels good, do it." "Look out for number one." "You're worth it." "I did it my way." These perspectives feed the flesh but do nothing to feed the soul.

The *San Francisco Chronicle* reports the following:

In fact, based on a *Chronicle* Poll of 600 adults that examines a new generation gap between the post–World War II baby boomers (ages 30 to 47) and the posties[1]—the post–Vietnam, post–modern Generation Xers (ages 18 to 29), those young hipsters aren't happy at all. Among the findings:

- Six in 10 posties say life is harder for them than their parents.
- Three in 20 posties think that most of the good jobs have already been taken.
- One in four female boomers says her life is very stressful, but nearly one in three describes herself as very happy.

"What we see is a combination of experiences related to age as well as frustration with the current state of our economy that has created more uncertainty than usual for people starting out," says *Chronicle* pollster Mark Baldassare.

"As a result we see the posties are a lot more concerned about achieving material things such as wealth and success," he says. "Boomers, on the other hand, are surprised at how well they have done. They're happy with their jobs and love life but—women in particular—wish they had a little more time for themselves."[2]

THE REAL ISSUE

Most of us, if we would admit it, spend a lot of time being angry at people who move too slowly, or at the ones who act cold and indifferent to us. I have found this to be true in dealing with my local Post Office clerk. I wonder, "Why won't you smile? What have I done to you?" She grabs my letters, stamps, and packages and walks away. My typical reaction has been to demonstrate my disappointment with a carefully directed glance or a well-timed sigh. This probably annoys her, but when she doesn't look, I get all the more irritated. She simply won't respond the way I want her to.

I remember deciding to try an experiment: The next time I went to the post office, I wouldn't be annoyed by her behavior. She was unhappy; I didn't have to be. Each time I went, I was cordial, I smiled and thanked her. Although she didn't change, I did and was able to handle her attitude in an uncritical way.

We are not helpless to change, but the comfort of staying the way we are is so great. After all, it appears easier to change the outside situations than to improve ourselves on the inside. Yet because of our feelings of inadequacy, we begin running faster and faster, searching for self-fulfillment.

This pattern of thinking keeps us stuck in a never-ending cycle of busyness, hurrying, and achieving. And once you gain momentum, the cycle is hard to break.

Let me explain how this works by showing you a simple schematic of the lure of the Rat Race.

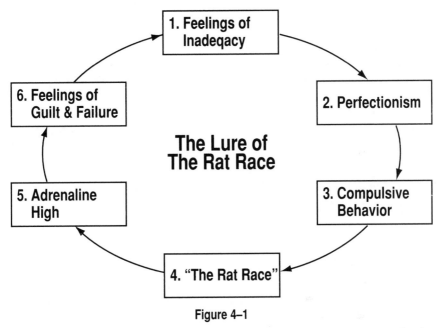

Figure 4–1

The cycle begins with an inherent desire to become somebody because you feel so inadequate now and thus insecure. You'll do anything to relieve the pain and fill the emptiness. Inevitably, perfectionist thinking becomes a way of life. Many people who are caught on the fast track contend that nothing they ever did as a child was good enough for their parents and teachers. Unfortunately, this pattern of thinking will become their tombstone if left unchecked as an adult. The answer seems to be: Do it right or don't do it at all. You never want to hear, "You're mediocre on the job." Your motto becomes this: Be the best at what you do. *I'll become the best father in the world. I'll be a millionaire by 40 ; then I'll have more time at home. I'm going to get straight A's. I want my parents to be proud of me.* We think that when we are the best, we can feel more secure and can feel significant and like we are somebody important. So if a person could find personal significance in doing things very well, it would be fine. God wants us to do the best we can. However, this does not solve the problem for most people, it only creates a new one, for the cycle continues as the perfectionist thinking causes us to bite off more than we can chew.

Sal and Mary (not their real names) found themselves in this cycle. Sal had two jobs, and he spent most of his day trying to keep up. His perfectionism pushed him to do better and better so that more time would be available to do even more.

Sal grew up with that mindset. From piano lessons to keeping his room neat, he always was "doing." He didn't stop until eleven or twelve o'clock at night. In college, his favorite courses started at 7:00 A.M., and he always arrived at least a half hour early. "I was always a model student, the teacher's pet, devastated if I were not the top of my class." Sal had compulsive behavior to do the most, and be the best. This made him an ideal candidate for the Rat Race.

Of course, his perfectionism affected his marriage as well. Sal shares, "I've always expected Mary to perform to my level of expectations and to my degree of perfection." Because of Sal's perfectionism and compulsiveness, he and Mary have decided not to have children. Though Mary accepts Sal unconditionally, they both feel their lifestyle would not be fair to children.

Does Sal need to change? I asked him this very question. He answered, "Glen, I'm not sure I can. I'm running as fast as I can, thinking as hard as I can, and still cannot meet my own standards. How can I get out of this Rat Race?" His question is not uncommon. The workplace can become a source of constant tension if balance is not found and equilibrium is not achieved.

Compulsive behavior eventually becomes a way of life. When things go well, an adrenaline high naturally follows. Producing and achieving temporarily fills the inner emptiness and gives a fleeting and false sense of fulfillment, at least until the next morning. Then you sadly awaken to the reality that the race is still on.

Feelings of failure and guilt follow. The fear of failure drives people to produce harder and harder. They take on mountains of "doing" even when their professional and personal lives are already overloaded. They tend to set themselves up for failure because their standards are so high that no one could ever meet them. And on the inside, they feel like a small child who never does anything right, harshly judging themselves for even the smallest failures and the slightest flaws. Their negative self-talk can be quite harmful, even emotionally crippling.

Young people are offered little counsel at home or in school concerning the vast possibilities for their lives. The classics have been replaced by business texts, engineering books, and scientific technology. Youth go to college to get a degree that will get them a job, not help them learn about themselves and the world in which they live. They graduate with a narrow degree which allows little flexibility in a specialized job market. Then they feel trapped in their jobs because they think, *this is all I've been trained do.*

Thus, we find fifty-five-year-old real estate brokers, forty-five-year-old engineers, thirty-five-year-old teachers, and twenty-five-year-old business people all asking, "Is this all there is to life?" They seemingly have it all with money—more than they had ever dreamed of. They are respected and admired by their peers. But there's something missing. And that missing "something" drives people to therapy, mid-life crises, and relationship breakdowns.

Can anything be done? It appears we only have three options: succumb, survive, or succeed. To succumb is to allow the ever changing values and influences of the Rat Race to change us and to allow the world to force us into its mold, missing much of what God has for us. To survive is to do only what we need to do to get by. It is to hide our heads in the sand hoping to hang on to what we have. Here, too, we miss God's best. But to succeed is to move forward in accomplishing our God-given mission in life for His glory.

TAKE YOUR JOB AND LOVE IT?!

I've always wondered what it would have been like to be one of the seven dwarfs heading off to work. (You can provide the whistling.) Smiles on their faces, excitement in their step, off to a meaningful day—in a diamond mine!! No wonder they were excited. No wonder only one of them was called "Grumpy." When was the last time you went off to work in your own diamond mine? Our jobs are typically not this lucrative. We wake up, drag ourselves out of bed listening to "all news radio," and jump into our car to face a long traffic jam on the way to work. Max Anders concludes, ". . . for many people, work is drudgery, a meaningless necessity. With little connection between their workplace and the rest of their life, their life slogan is TGIF. Even Paul Harvey begins his Friday broadcast with, 'Good morning America, it's Friday.'"[3] Is it really possible to earn a living and make a life—to honestly enjoy my work?

LEARNING FROM HISTORY

A careful look at the changes which have occurred in the past fifty years will shed light on why our work has become a Rat Race rather than a source of fulfillment. We are in an age of change. Sociologists have determined that three distinct generations have shaped America over the last one hundred years.

The Pre-Boomers

The first generation, we'll call them the "pre-boomers,"[4] were born prior to 1946. As difficult as it was, they made the transition from an agricultural era to the age of industrialization. Their lives were shaped by the struggles of the twenties through the forties. They were proud to say that they were the generation that had overcome two world wars, the Great Depression, and a host of technological advances each of which was monumental in its day.

Three words describe this generation: saving, loyal, and working. The pre-boomers saved everything because they never knew if they would need it in the future. They were the loyal generation. They stayed in the same job, the same company, and the same church for the better part of their lives. They were extremely loyal to their friends as well. The pre-boomers had to band together to survive the Great Depression and the War. When they made a friend, it was often for life. Their work ethic permeated everything they did: "If a job is worth doing, it is worth doing well." On the job, they handled authority in the same way as the military had instructed them—with respect. The pre-boomers rarely questioned their superiors; when they were told to do something, their reply was, "Yes, Sir!"

The Baby Boomers

The baby-boom generation grew up in an entirely different economic climate and society. Pre-boomers gave their boomer children everything that post–war prosperity and unprecedented economic growth had to offer. Advertisers caught on quickly and immediately made boomers the targets of everything from yo-yo's to hula-hoops.

Boomers are the generation who challenged everything, became highly educated, and sacrificed family for career. From his personal boomer perspective, Doug Murren outlines nine characteristics that make boomers so special:

- We're the first generation to be raised, by and large, with absentee fathers.
- We're also the first generation whose grandparents had no significant input in terms of life preparation and wage-earning skills.
- We're the most educated generation in history.
- We were raised in extreme affluence, with opportunities unimaginable to our parents.
- We came into childhood and adolescence at the time of the greatest economic expansion in world history.
- We're the first generation who can't afford to maintain what we've always had.
- We're the first generation raised under the near-constant threat of nuclear war.
- We're the first generation to be reared with television as a significant parenting tool. [5]

By saying they challenged everything, I'm merely saying that their experience with the military and government was not as positive as that of their predecessors. Boomers had seen the escalation of a "police action" turn into a Vietnam, and they had witnessed Watergate, the greatest scandal to hit the White House.

The boomers are also highly educated. Nearly one quarter of all boomers have earned a college degree, compared with only nine percent of those people over sixty-five.[6] It is because of this education and subsequent surge into an informational age that, "American society has become more diverse and non-accepting of diversity." [7]

Boomers are the generation labeled as DINKS, "Double Income No Kids." Children weren't abandoned; they were just left "home alone." Latchkey kids were common in the lower and middle classes, while the upper class boomers left their children in the capable hands of coaches and teachers—ballet, soccer, piano, the list goes on. Boomers were not savers like their parents; they saw little need for saving. However, as the baby boomers have reached middle age, concern for the future of social security, retirement, and the planet has captured more of their attention.

Their work ethic is highly characteristic of the Rat Race. The typical boomer, brought up in the fast-paced environment of the sixties, is success -oriented, highly pressured, and becoming intense in an age of "down-sizing." In their middle age, they are sensing the need for continual education to keep up with the technology. Where the agrarian lifestyle was consistent, the informational lifestyle of today is in a constant state of flux—and so are the boomers. So, they are continually questioning the motives of others as well as their own personal priorities. Thus, when they are told to do something on the job, their reply is, "Why?"

The Baby Busters

The third generation, the "busters," is only just now rising to prominence and impacting our culture. Growing up in a variable economy and a seemingly limitless expansion in communication and technology, they are facing three dynamic roadblocks.

The first roadblock is affordable education. Data from 1988 was analyzed by Doug Murren in his book, *The Baby Boomerang*: "Two years ago colleges graduated only eight percent more graduates while the job market had room for twenty-five percent."[8] As optimistic as this sounds, pessimism is often the reality as the soaring costs of education and poor parental financial planning hinders their dreams. One buster, who graduated at the top of her class, said, "I can't see graduating in four years and immediately going to graduate school. My undergraduate work will likely take five years and I will be so far in debt, I'll probably have to get a job to start the long road to recovery."

The second roadblock centers around the busters' need for continual change. Even at their young age, busters are highly mobile, and most are single. They enjoy moving from project to project and place to place. This is most likely fueled by their short attention span that was created by the media environment in which they grew up. This generation not only anticipates the Rat Race, but enjoys its hectic pace. To them, life seems mundane if it moves slowly, but because it is often so fast, they have also found it to be unfulfilling.

The last roadblock the busters will overcome is the work place. Due to their mobility, busters find it extremely easy to move from job to job, searching for the illusive perfect work place with the right benefits. Their main concern is not loyalty to the company, but the job which will best meet their needs and give them a reason to work. If the job does not do those two things, they will need to find another; they will not typically sell their life to a company. The busters' work ethic, therefore, falls in between the pre-boomers and the boomers. When they are presented with a task, such as an assignment at work, they will most likely think, "What's in it for me?" And if you, the boss, do not answer correctly, they begin updating their résumé.

FIVE PILLARS TO A SATISFYING PROFESSION

Let me share some interesting pieces of trivia. *In One Day:* 1 American is injured by lightning; 104 are injured while shaving; Americans eat 24,657,534 hot dogs; Americans purchase 3,014 hockey sticks; 4 Americans call Graceland asking to speak to Elvis; and 8 out of 10 complain about their job.[9]

This cycle of work-complain-work-complain does not have to be the norm as we will discover through the five pillars for job satisfaction as shown in the following diagram.

Figure 4–2

The Foundation. The Bible is filled with promises, hundreds of demonstrations of God's faithfulness and love for His children. Often, God ties His promises to some action on our part. God says to us, "When you do this . . . I will do that." Proverbs 16:3 reminds us to "commit to the Lord whatever you do, and your plans will succeed." Solomon also wrote in Proverbs 3:5-6, "Trust in the Lord with all your heart and lean not on your own understanding; in all your ways acknowledge him, and he will make your paths straight."

Looking at these two passages of Scripture, your part to play in the equation is to "commit to the Lord whatever you do," and "trust in the Lord with all your heart." How can you do this in the work place? What steps must you take to make the transition from a job in the Rat Race to a work that is both pleasing to your Creator and fulfilling to you?

Pillar #1 — Purpose. Many times, the difference between fulfillment and exasperation in the workplace is a sense of purpose. Sherman and Hendricks note, "many workers in the modern marketplace feel increasingly bored with their jobs and with life. This is the subtext of all the glitzy beer, hamburger, and travel commercials that show hardworking laborers building America and solving its problems. They portray the workplace not as it is but as we wish it could be—an engrossing, challenging, even uplifting human drama in which each of us performs our strategic role and fulfills a personal mission. Instead, for many work is 'just a job.' Its value begins and ends with a paycheck." [10]

Your work is not a prison, but it will seem that way without a purpose. The Lord Jesus had a purpose. Even as a young man He said, "I must be about My Father's business." (Luke 2:49, NKJV) The apostle Paul had a purpose. He told the church in Philippi, "But one thing I do . . ." (Phil. 3:13). He didn't say, "These ten things I dabble in." Paul had a clear purpose. God may give us the ingredients for our daily bread, but He expects us to do the baking.

Never forget that work was God's idea. Genesis 1:27–28 reminds us, "So God created man in his own image, in the image of God he created him; male and female he created them. God blessed them and said to them, 'Be fruitful and increase in number; fill the earth and subdue it. Rule over the fish of the sea and the birds of the air and over every living creature that moves on the ground." The key, however, to enjoying this work is our purpose and perspective. Yes, I work to pay the bills and provide security for the ones I love. Yes, I work to give myself the wonderful opportunity to give and support others in the Lord's work. But ultimately I work for the Lord. Colossians 3:23 says, "Whatever you do, work at it with all your heart, as working for the Lord, not for men." Working for the Lord doesn't happen just while you are at church, but wherever He puts you. And when you see the real purpose—serving God—as the reason for working, you have the beginnings of a satisfying work environment.

Pillar #2 – Character. Earl Palmer has written a timely book titled *Integrity in a World of Pretense.* He devotes his book to studying human nature as presented by the apostle Paul in the Book of Philippians. I love Palmer's conclusion: "Integrity is not a matter of doing or not doing certain things. It is a way of life. It affects everything we do, from the big, life-changing decisions we must make to the small, incidental encounters in the supermarket. When we try to reduce it to a simple set of rules we have missed the point." [11] Bill Hybels shares, "Character, a wise person said, is what we do when no one is looking. It is not the same as reputation—what other people think of us. It is not the same as success or achievement. Character is not what we have done, but who we are."[12]

Let's make this issue of character practical to our work place with a few illustrations.

- As salespeople, we don't lie or deceive people to get the sale.
- As employers, we make sure that those who work for us are adequately compensated and fairly treated.
- We don't steal pencils, paper, or other supplies from the work place.
- We don't make excuses for our personal mistakes.
- We don't waste time on the job, even if it is for "spiritual" reasons.
- We arrive on time and clock out appropriately.

This list is endless and must be personalized to your work situation. But remember, the Bible tells us, "The man of integrity walks securely, but he who takes crooked paths will be found out" (Prov. 10:9).

Pillar #3 — Education. Have you ever met someone who was convinced that his education was over the moment he graduated from high school or college? When you stop learning, you stop growing and developing. We must be in constant search of wisdom and knowledge. Solomon wrote hundreds of years ago, "The discerning heart seeks knowledge, but the mouth of a fool feeds on folly," (Prov. 15:14). In other words, we must never be satisfied with ignorance, or with what

Gordon MacDonald calls "mental flabbiness." He writes, "In our pressurized society, people who are out of shape mentally usually fall victim to ideas and systems that are destructive to the human spirit and to human relationships. They are victimized because they have not taught themselves how to think, nor have they set themselves to the life-long pursuit of the growth of the mind. Not having the facility of a strong mind, they grow dependent upon the thoughts and opinions of others. Rather than deal with ideas and issues, they reduce themselves to lives full of rules, regulations, and program."[13]

Just as growing churches need leaders who are growing, growing businesses need business who are growing and growing relationships need the commitment to learn and grow. "Failure is the path of least persistence."[14]

So, where do you learn? Let's look at four possibilities. First, learn from the Bible. In 2 Timothy 3:16–17 Paul clearly says, "All Scripture is God-breathed and is useful for teaching, rebuking, correcting and training in righteousness, so that the man of God may be thoroughly equipped for every good work." If God's will is found in God's Word, doesn't it make sense to make the Bible a priority?

Second, we can learn from our failures. We are told concerning the exploits of Joshua, "Be strong and very courageous. Be careful to obey all the law my servant Moses gave you; do not turn from it to the right or to the left, that you may be successful wherever you go" (Josh. 1:7). Joshua is told by God to stay on track, but you know as well as I do that failures are a part of life, and we must be willing to learn from them.

Joshua chapter 7 has a great example. Joshua and the troops came to the little town of Ai. Everything had been going well; Jericho had been defeated. But the people became overconfident, and the Israelites failed to capture the city. Joshua wasn't handling the defeat very well and God confronted him in Joshua 7:10, "The LORD said to Joshua, 'Stand up! What are you doing down on your face?'" So Joshua found out about the sin in his camp and dealt with Achan and his failure to follow God's rules. From that point on, there was victory. Why? Because when we fail, we must deal with the reason, take action, learn, and move on.

The third area from which we can learn from is godly counsel. Proverbs 15:22 exhorts us, "Plans fail for lack of counsel, but with many advisers they succeed." Now remember, this godly counsel can also come in the form of criticism. Again in Proverbs, chapter 13, verse 18, "He who ignores discipline comes to poverty and shame, but whoever heeds correction is honored." Criticism if warranted can be very helpful if it is handled well. If the criticism is unwarranted, commit it to the Lord and do as Moses did—pray and move on.

Finally, we can take advantage of learning opportunities at work or in our community. Does your company offer classes or other assistance that will help you update or expand your skills? Is there a college or a community college in your area that offers classes that could prepare you for advancement or career change?

Pillar #4 — Time. I don't want to spend too much time on this particular issue because chapter 8 is solely devoted to the subject of learning to control your time. But I wonder how long it has been since you said to yourself, "Where did my time go?" We all have the same amount given to us, but not everyone uses it wisely. Psalm 90:12 says, "Teach us to number our days aright, that we may gain a heart of wisdom." There appears to be added wisdom given to the person who is skilled in time management. For without the correct use of time, our work is disorganized, our families suffer, and life appear to be out of control.

Pillar #5 — Persistence. Stephen Covey, in *The 7 Habits of Highly Effective People*, challenges his readers to think in a new paradigm for renewal, "The Upward Spiral."[15] He depicts the renewal that is necessary to maintain longevity as an upward spiral of learning, committing, and doing. He writes, "I believe that as we grow and develop on this upward spiral, we must show diligence in the process of renewal by educating and obeying our conscience. An increasingly educated conscience will propel us along the path of personal freedom, security, wisdom, and power.

"Moving along the upward spiral requires us to *learn, commit,* and *do* on increasingly higher planes. We deceive ourselves if we think that any one of these is sufficient. To keep progressing, we must learn, commit, and do—learn, commit, and do-and learn, commit, and do again."[16] Covey portrays life, growth, and achievement as merely a process—a process which will need your stamina to be completed.

THE RIGHT PERSPECTIVE

Your work can be enjoyable. The key is your perspective. I love the way Doug Sherman says it: "But unlike those who only work for their own ego gratification, you have a higher calling. Work, as God intended it, is a gift from the Lord to bring glory to Him. It is a gift, a high honor that you have your job. The psalmist says, 'When I consider your heavens, the work of your fingers, the moon and the stars, which you have set in place, what is man that you are mindful of him, the son of man that you care for him? You made him a little lower than the heavenly beings and crowned him with glory and honor. You made him ruler over the works of your hands; you put everything under his feet' (Ps. 8:3–6).[17]

"But the point of this high calling is to bring glory to God, not ourselves. Thus your focus and perspective at work should be to bring glory to God by the way you do your work. Your integrity, the excellence you bring to your job, your ambition, and the quality of your peer relationships can all reflect the glory of the Savior."[18]

Paul echoes this truth in his own way in Philippians 1:20 and 3:14 when he says, "I eagerly expect and hope that I will in no way be ashamed, but will have sufficient courage so that now as always Christ will be exalted in my body, whether by life or by death. . . . I press on toward the goal to win the prize for which God has called me heavenward in Christ Jesus."

When we have all five elements of the pillars securely in place, built upon the commitment of our work to the Lord, there is no way we can *not* have real job satisfaction. Because of the key role that work plays in the Rat Race, when we have job satisfaction, we are well on our way to avoiding the lure, detours, and traps of the Rat Race. We can stay in God's Royal Race all the way. Even in the midst of the Rat Race, we can maintain our right perspective by staying in the center of the narrow road on which He has placed us. In this way, we will avoid the, the chaos of the Rat Race. We will cover this in more detail in chapter 5.

Yet, I can just hear some of you saying, "Has anyone really been able to make it? Is this really a doable thing?" What great questions! Let's see if we can find the answers in the next chapter.

Chapter Five

Surviving the Rat Race

"I have found the road to success no easy matter," said a modern business executive to an interviewer. "I started at the bottom. I worked fourteen hours a day. I sweated. I fought. I maneuvered. I schemed. I took abuse. I did things others might not approve of. But I kept on climbing the ladder."

" And now, of course, you are a success?" prompted the interviewer.

"No, I wouldn't say that," replied the business executive. "Just quote me as saying that I have become an expert at climbing ladders."[1]

It has been said that to succeed in this complex, modern age, a person has to keep his back to the wall, his ear to the ground, his shoulder to the wheel, his nose to the grindstone and both feet on the ground. Undoubtedly this is a good formula for becoming a pretzel or becoming an expert at climbing ladders. However, if you aspire to genuine success, with lasting value and ultimate meaning, you must do more than keep your ear to the ground, your shoulder to the wheel, and your nose to the grindstone—you must keep your eyes on the Lord and your heart in the Lord's service. This is God's formula for successful balance in a chaotic world.

Three Main Roads

The following diagram shows the three main roads on which we as believers can be in our "life race." The ideal one is the Royal Road. It is the road, which if followed carefully, will lead the runner in the best path possible towards the goal the Lord has for him. As we will see chapter 12, there is even a life map that God has uniquely designed for believers to follow as they run their race. When accurately followed, it will lead to winning the prize at the end of the race. A runner may get pulled onto the Rat Race through a detour, but he can get back to God's Royal Road if he follows God's instructions.

For some, however, the Rat Race is the only option. This is true for mothers of small children, those who are in higher levels of the business world, and people who must work more than one job or long hours just to supply necessities (not just desires). For them, God's Royal Road is in the middle of the Rat Race, which I call the "eye of the storm." This is the narrow road that Christ speaks of in Matthew 7:14. God can provide calm and joy in the midst of their storms if they carefully live their lives under His guidance, keeping their minds focused on Him and not on their circumstances. They can be like the one who is in the eye of the storm—at perfect peace, even with everything in chaos around him.

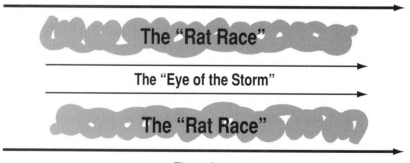

Figure 5–1

God has a sworn adversary who wants to destroy everything that is precious to the Lord. Satan is jealous of God's love for humanity. Satan's hatred for God is strongly expressed in his desire to stop the Lord's plans for humankind; he does everything he can to defeat, trick, intimidate, and lie to humans. If Satan finds he cannot keep us from serving God, then he will try to detour us into the world's Rat Race. The diagram below gives a feel for how this happens.

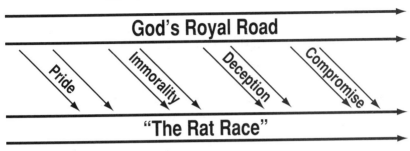

Figure 5–2

There are several different detours that Satan has devised to tempt us to leave God's Royal Road. Some of these include the road to fame, the road to riches, and the road to power and influence. But when he cannot get us to take one of these roads, he then pulls out his most deceptive detour, the detour of good works. This one is easily disguised as the road to doing good things for God and others. It is a road that leads to the Rat Race and to burn out. This road looks good and even feels good, but inevitably it leads to frustration, disappointment, and even disaster.

Beware! The Enemy uses his detour as a clever trap to bog down believers in things that dilute their effectiveness for the Lord. It is a giant spider web with many sticky strings. Often the more the believers struggle to escape, the deeper they get entangled. Despair and feelings of hopelessness are the usual results. And apart from God, there is no real hope to be free from many of the negative aspects of following a detour.

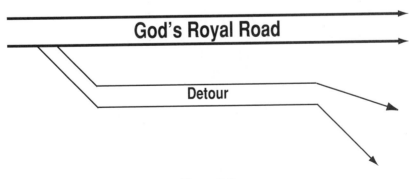

Figure 5–3

You will notice that on this detour, there is a nice wide entrance to the side road. It has pleasant scenery that appeals to us such as people in need, good deeds to do, ways to feel important, and so on.

All of these detours lead downward. None lead up or are even parallel to God's road. Oh to be sure, they start out almost parallel, maybe only a half a degree off but they are off. The further you go, the more evident it is that something is not quite right. You may not be able to put your finger on it at first, but in time you will come to realize that you have gotten off the Royal Road and are off base, off target. You are missing your mark and are being pulled in a wrong direction. You have lost your peace, your joy, and maybe even your meaning and direction in life.

So how do we identify detours? How do we know the road we are on is the one God has for us?

There are six rules, which if followed, will help guarantee we will stay on God's Royal Road, and that we will avoid the detours and traps of the Rat Race.

RULES FOR THE ROYAL ROAD

1. Have a good relationship with God. In order to hear from God and to receive His direction in our lives, we have to have a personal relationship with Him. This occurs when we recognize our sin; and acknowledge that Jesus is God's provision for our sin, ask Jesus to come into our life, forgive our sins, take over every area of our life, and make us what He wants us to be. At this point we become a child of God.

Just as any child needs to grow physically to be healthy, so we need to grow spiritually in our relationship with God. Our spiritual food is the Word of God and our fellowship comes as we talk to God in prayer. Combining these two creates a deepening relationship with Him as we share our heart and learn to listen to Him.

2. Develop complete faith and trust in God. As we study the Word and pray, we will see many truths about God and His nature. Combining these with our own experience of Him will help us develop a strong faith and trust in His guidance. This is necessary if we are to stay on the Royal Road. Just as the enemy did with Eve, so will he try to tempt us to leave God's way and make us distrust Him. Faith and trust are especially necessary when roadblocks, such as temptations, come.

3. Seek God in all areas of our lives and obey what He shows. When we run our race, we must be certain to let God guide us in everything. No successful runner would listen to the coach only about exercise and strategy and ignore his advice on eating and sleeping. Submission and obedience to the coach are necessary in all areas. So it is in our spiritual race. We need God's insight and instructions in every area of our lives and to follow them exactly if we want to finish our race well. Only He knows the Enemy's plans and can help us avoid the detours and obstacles.

4. Live under the control of the Holy Spirit moment by moment. No one driving on a race track at high speeds dares become careless. In order to avoid "accidents" in our lives, we must stay alert, seeking to live under the Lord's control every moment. This is such an important area that we will look at it in depth in chapter 3.

5. Be aware of the possible Enemy detours and traps he has placed in our path. In war, the military commander does everything he can to know his enemy and the tactics he uses. Only in this way can he avoid enemy traps. This one element greatly increases the commander's chance to win the war. As believers, we are in a type of "race war"—not a social one, but a spiritual one. We need to know that the Enemy does not want us on God's Royal Road. He wants us caught in the Rat Race.

6. Recognize that we are in a time of training with Him. Unlike a physical race, our spiritual race is more like on the job training. We are in the race at the same time that we are receiving training. Our life skills are being improved, our times of study get deeper as we go along, and the tests and trials that come our way challenge us to be all we can be and to look to our Lord even more.

We are always in the race. The question is which course will we be on. As we apply these six principles for faithfully following God's guidance, we will be actively involved in successfully running on God's Royal Road. The course is not an easy one, but the rewards are well worth the effort, both during the race and at the end.

Jesus wants us to be like Him. We are running the race to become like the One we serve. In Matthew 10:25, Jesus tells us, "It is enough for the student to be like his teacher." Then in Luke 6:40, He explains further, "After he has been fully trained, he will be like his teacher (NASB)."

Dallas Willard puts it this way: "Given this desire (to be like Jesus) usually produced by the lives and words of those already in The Way, there is yet a decision to be made: The disciple is one who, intent upon becoming Christ like and so dwelling in his 'faith and practice,' systematically and progressively rearranges his affairs to that end. By these actions, even today, one enrolls in Christ's training, becomes his pupil or disciple. There is no other way."[2]

Jesus is also on the road on which God has placed us. He is beside us, coaching us, helping us become like Him. But if we choose to take a detour or get caught in the Enemy traps, we will not be walking where He is and will not become like Him. It is our choice. But God has not left us without help or without instructions on how to stay in the center of the all important Royal Road. We have looked at the six principles He has given us. Now let's look at them in practice.

TWO WOMEN WITH DIFFERENT RESPONSES

The Bible has a beautiful way of letting us see the humanness of its people. Let me use the Martin Amplified Version of Luke 10:38–42 to illustrate how two sisters reacted when tempted by the Rat Race.[3]

The scene might have gone this way: The time is about two thousand years ago. It is a hot, dusty day in the village of Bethany. Jesus and His disciples have been ministering much of the day. As they travel, they decide to drop by the home of Martha. Because there were no phones, most likely their arrival is unexpected but most welcomed. Since it is mealtime, Martha swings into high gear to prepare her dear, hungry friends a wonderful feast with all the trimmings. Everything must be perfect for the Master. However, with no refrigeration, everything has to be done from scratch. With at least thirteen people to feed, this is no small task. Martha's sister, Mary, is there, but to Martha's consternation, Mary has not volunteered to help her prepare this meal. She has instead chosen to listen to Jesus as He teaches.

Let's eavesdrop on what might have been going through Martha's mind that hot day.

I can't believe it. First I get this unexpected crowd for lunch. Obviously I have to have the very best feast I can for my dear friend and His companions. It must be perfect. At least my sister's here, so she could pitch in and help if she wanted to. But will she? Oh, no. When I asked her, she refused, saying we could fix something simple, not the fancy meal I've planned. Naturally, I rejected such a crazy idea.

So Mary trots off to the living room, saying she wants to listen to Jesus. And my dear, thoughtful sister leaves everything for me to do. It's not right. I'd like to be there, doing nothing but listening to Jesus. He's my friend, too. Why doesn't she come and help me fix this feast so I can get finished sooner? It's really unfair. Jesus is a fair person. I'm going to ask Him to make her help me. Goodness knows, I've helped her many times when she had company at her home. Little sisters! What ungrateful people they can be at times.

As the story unfolds, we find Martha going to Jesus, complaining about Mary and asking Him to make her help. Jesus' answer astounds Martha.

And now, of all things, I've asked Jesus to make Mary do the right thing, and He says she is doing not only the right thing, but the best thing, for she has chosen to listen to Him. He says I'm "worried and upset about many things, but only one thing is needed and Mary has chosen it." It hurt to hear Him say this, especially as pressured, upset, and nervous as this has made me. But now that I think about it, I guess He is right. Food is something we always need, and whether they eat a big, fancy meal or a small, simple one will not make much difference when compared to hearing my Friend teach the wonderful truths of God. I guess I really need to have the right perspective and value on the events of life and choose those things which have a meaning for eternity, as Mary has. Wish I had accepted her input at the first about the meal and saved myself all this frustration and embarrassment. O.K. Simple it is! And I'll get to hear Him teach some, myself.

Most of us have no trouble understanding the story of Mary and Martha. I can easily identify with Martha's desire to have everything "just right" for her important guests. She cared about them, was devoted to Jesus and wanted to be the perfect hostess. Her diligence and devotion drove her to want to be in complete control of the situation, to do things the way she thought best, and in turn, to have the help of those whom she felt also should feel the same way, namely her sister. My bet is that Martha was the older sister who was used to having Mary's help and was a little taken aback when Mary wanted to do what she felt was best.

Those caught in the Rat Race often have myopia. They can only see what they want, not the bigger picture. Once they get started in one direction, they tend to go for it with all they have, and can leave some wounded or neglected people on the way. This is what often happens with the man who is highly successful in business but a failure as a husband and father. His tunnel vision aimed only at his business success can cause him to lose the very things for which he is working. Isn't this to some degree what Martha was doing? She was so busy working for her Lord, that she didn't have time to be with Him. Her tunnel vision let her see only one acceptable way of feeding this group, even though there may have been several options available. When we start going our own way and not seeking God's perspective in a situation, we can get into trouble.

The busy housewife can be as guilty of neglecting her family's emotional needs as the successful businessman. If she is not careful, she can easily ignore her children or be too busy to listen to them or spend time in talking with them because she is stressed out from doing the many physical activities of a mother and housewife. Her husband may also feel neglected because she is too exhausted to spend any time with him by the time he gets home. On the weekends she has a million things for him to do around the house, none of which include some quality, quiet time with him just talking or doing fun things together. Her husband may notice, but may not act on his responsibility to suggest a change because he, too, is near the breaking point in his Rat Race. Both have lost God's perspective by not bringing Him into their usage of time and in decision making.

We too often think that seeking God's will is reserved for the major decisions in our life. It is this, but it is much more. I love the way Dr. Jim Judge puts it, "It's not just a one-time decision we make, . . . It's the hundreds of decisions we make every day."[4] Martha's decision was a simple one, it seemed. Not the kind we usually think we need to pray about. And yet it was important enough to be recorded in the Bible for everyone to read and learn from.

So what are we to learn? One of the important things the Lord wants us to see is that sometimes small decisions we make can have an impact for eternity. There are no small decisions in our lives. Everything we do should be done with the thought in mind of does it count for eternity? Not all things do, not all things need to. But where there is a choice between those that do count for eternity and those that do not, God's perspective is to choose those with eternal value. This is why Jesus commends Mary because "Mary has chosen what is better, and it will not be taken away from her." Did Martha learn her lesson this time? Who knows! For in John 12:1–3 we again see a dinner given in Jesus' honor with Martha serving and Mary taking a box of ointment and pouring it on His feet.

Following God's six basic principles for our lives and thus avoiding many of the traps of the Rat Race is not just a nice thing to do. It really is a necessity if you are to function as God intends and fulfill all God has for your life.

So, How Are You Doing?

How are you doing in following the six principles in your life that God has laid out as a road map for you? If you are finding that you've taken a detour or are close to doing so, you might want to pray a prayer similar to the following:

> Lord, You know my heart. I want to follow only Your plan for my life, to be on Your Royal Road and to avoid all the detours and temptations of the Enemy. Please show me any point at which I have gone away from the center of your plans for me, have bought into an Enemy lie, and thus taken a detour. Show me what I need to do to get back to where You want me to be. Holy Spirit, show me how to stay on Your path for my life and how to avoid future detours and traps. Lord Jesus, help me keep all my thoughts under Your control and to recognize and therefore resist any that are not from You. I want to run the race You have for me, Father, and to win the prize at the end. Do in my life what You need to in order to accomplish that end. I trust You. Help me to trust You even more.

When you can sincerely pray a prayer like this, you will be well on your way to being victorious in walking on God's path for your life and avoiding the many detours and traps of the Rat Race.

It's time now to go back to the seven warning signs of the Rat Race and learn what we can do to overcome each of those dangers.

PART THREE

Seven Steps to Moving Beyond the Rat Race

Chapter Six

Learn Your Limits

I am not the man I used to be. I no longer enjoy playing loud video games; they now make me dizzy. I love coaching my daughter's softball team and my son's baseball teams, but I no longer play third base on the church's softball team. I used to stay up until midnight or one o'clock with regularity, studying and writing, but I've found that as I have "matured" (this is the baby boomers' terminology for aging), I need at least seven hours of sleep or I will be a waste the following day. All this to say, I'm learning my limits, which will help prevent warning sign number one, brownout.

One of the reasons we get trapped in the Rat Race is because we have not learned to set limits. Many of us don't even know what our limits are. In fact, we don't even like limitations. We see them as confining and the result of personal weakness. However, learning our limits will prevent much of the pain of brownouts the first warning sign of a life trapped in the Rat Race. Dallas Willard shares a great insight in his book *In Search of Guidance*, "We all live at the mercy of our ideas."[1] These ideas affect every area of our lives—from our relationship with God to our relationship with those we love on earth.

Seven Problem Thoughts

Learning your limits implies that you have learned something about the real you. The tendency of people who struggle with the Rat Race lifestyle is to begin doubting their capabilities and strengths by questioning everything else from relationships to career. There are seven patterns of thinking that will cause problems because those involved have overextended their personal expectations and limits.

Thought #1 — "**I must be approved or loved by everyone.**" We all want to be loved. This is a natural desire. Love is a powerful motivator, but we must remain rational. We are not to sacrifice our own interests and desires in search of total and complete acceptance by everyone we meet. The healthiest way to experience love is to allow God to be the primary source of your love. Let His direct love for you be what satisfies your heart and let His indirect love as shown through others be an added dimension of His loving you. In this way, you look to Him to supply your needs—yes, even your need for love and acceptance. Others always disappoint us and fall below our expectations. When we look to others to meet our needs, we leave ourselves wide open for the hurt which inevitably comes.

I speak to pastors across the country every year. I have heard just about every complaint, every heartbreaking story, and every definition of the church. I have heard the church called a hospital and an army. I've even heard a compromise of the two—a MASH unit. A pastor in Oregon once said that preaching in his church was like "preaching to a parade." A parade? Now think about this analogy. People come and people go. Ours is a transient society with people moving about every three to five years. Maybe he's right. But the sad part of the story lies in the fact that this pastor was very discouraged. Some of the people relocated because of jobs. Others were simply not happy with his style and vision and went on to other churches. His discouragement was based upon his inability to please everyone. Our security and significance come from our relationship with Christ. He alone has promised never to leave us or forsake us. As long as we that know we are pleasing Him, what others think becomes secondary.

The best way I can illustrate this is to have you imagine the will of the Father as a plumb line for your life. Once you know for certain what God's will is for any given situation, follow what He shows you. If someone wants you to go his way—veer to the right or left of the plumb line—you can know that person is trying to pull you away from what God wants you to do. Taking this perspective can relieve a lot of pressure as you take your directions from the Lord and not from the people around you, who can never be satisfied anyway.

Thought #2 — "I must continually be striving to be the best in order to be happy." If this describes you today, it is a good thing you didn't have this philosophy when you were learning to walk, to talk, or to ride a bike. People with such a philosophy should hang up their car keys when they get their first ticket or have their first accident.

There is nothing wrong with wanting to do well, whether it be for your own sake or to gain the recognition of others. The problems arise when our desires focus entirely upon excelling above others. We forget to enjoy the activity and thus engage in work and recreation solely for the results. Our goal is perfection rather than education or skill development.

I teach at Biola University in the Talbot School of Theology. I only have time to teach one course, but it is one I thoroughly enjoy—Christian Ethics. I teach this class using a spirit of cooperation rather than competition. At first, students tend to be a little reluctant. In their group assignments, they may fear that another person will not contribute and thus adversely affect their grade. But by the end of the semester, a bond forms, and they have a healthy reliance upon their teammates. In contrast, the modern educational structure is based upon percentages that usually follow a bell curve pattern. Competition says, "I've got to be on the left side of the curve, no matter who may be on the other side." Cooperation says, "Let's work together on this project recognizing that our product will be superior when we work together as a team." In the five years I've taught this class using the team format, every team says they learn more through the team style of teaching.

We must learn to redefine success. Success does not always mean the highest pay, the highest grade, or the highest degree. Success means learning from your mistakes and growing through them. If I always have to be the best and am afraid to try anything in which there is the possibility of failure, I would never try anything. That would be the greatest mistake of all.

God does want us to strive to be the best, but not in order to be happy, because He knows that true, lasting happiness cannot come only from our accomplishments. People who focus on accomplishments as their source and standard of happiness are doomed to be ruled by circumstances for the rest of their lives. Our happiness needs to be centered in God, in who we are in Him, in knowing that He is approving of us even when we make mistakes. Give yourself the freedom to fail. God does.

Thought #3 — "I must blame others for my mistakes so that I can get ahead." All of us make mistakes. No one, apart from the Lord Jesus Christ, is infallible. Blaming others for personal mistakes or bad decisions will never accomplish what we subconsciously hope for. Blame will never lead to improved behavior. Blame will never result in less stupidity, on your part or that of the other person. Blame will never manufacture more intelligence or a better, more balanced, emotional state. People who are in touch with reality admit their mistakes, accept them, and will not allow the mistakes to become a catastrophe or lead them to feel worthless.

Thought #4 — "Life is terrible when things are not going the way I want them to." When our lives revolve around ourselves—our wants, our desires, our plans—we are vulnerable to falling into the trap of self-centeredness and its resulting dissatisfaction. Two self-centered people will seldom be satisfied in any given situation because one of them may have his goals or desires blocked by the other. That is why God wants us to be centered on Him, not on ourselves or our circumstances. Only when we realize that He alone can satisfy us, and can make sense out of our lives, can we rest in Him when things don't go the way we thought they would.

Paul gave his whole life to sharing the Gospel, yet he often found himself in difficult positions—shipwrecked, beaten, imprisoned. He could have said, "Why aren't things going more smoothly? I'm doing God's will, and following His plan." But he didn't let events determine his feelings. He says in Philippians 4:11, "I have learned to be content whatever the circumstances." The Philippian believers would have known the truth of this statement. For in their very own jail, when Paul and Barnabas were also sitting with their feet chained in stocks and bleeding from a beating, they were praying and singing hymns!

We, too, need to forget about the circumstances and recognize that God is in the midst of all that is happening. He is in control of our lives and our circumstances. We also need to see if there is something we desire that is not in God's will—that is off the plumb line. God may be using this seemingly negative circumstance to correct our walk with Him and get us back on track. It is much easier to correct your course before you get sidetracked or actually trapped in the Rat Race than after the fact. Truly an ounce of God's prevention is worth a pound of our cure!

Thought #5 — I have to do whatever I see that needs to be done or whatever others ask of me. One of the great traps of the Enemy is to get us so busy—so tied up in doing, doing, doing that we have no time for God, for our family, for rest, or for other important things in life. This is one reason God so clearly tells us that He is there for us, helping us sort out the good from the best. It is true that I can do all things through Christ who strengthens me, but it is also true that I am not supposed to try to do everything. In Psalm 46:10, God says to us, "Be still and know that I am God." We are to quiet our hearts before Him. When we do this we can then trust in the Lord with all our hearts and He will direct our path (Prov. 3:5).

One look at the life of Jesus shows us that He did not do everything there was to do. Only one of the many sick at the pool of Bethesda was healed by Him, only one was even offered the opportunity for healing. Why didn't He do more? Because he said, "I do only what I see my Father do." He had learned to seek the Father in prayer, to get His instructions for the day, and then to do only those things that the Father had for Him to do. In the same way, we need to seek the Father, hear from Him what He wants us to do, and then when a new task presents itself to be done, do it only after consulting the Father and hearing from Him that this is to be part of the agenda for the day. By so doing, we will save ourselves the stress and pressure of taking on much more than the Lord ever meant us to have.

Thought #6 — "There are many things to fear in life and I dwell upon them continually." Life is complicated. It is unpredictable. Fear is one of the basic tools of the Enemy; he uses it in many ways. It can be either focused on something specific that threatens us, or be a generalized fear of the unknown. We can be paralyzed by unreasonable fears and thus become caught in one of the strong traps of the Rat Race.

Those who try to live life apart from the Lord indeed will find it a fearful, overwhelming prospect. They are alone and vulnerable to anything and everything. But those who trust in the Lord and have their minds fixed upon Him will have the perfect peace that we are promised in Isaiah 26:3. What problem is larger than the Lord? What problem is too complicated for Him to solve? Ask yourself the next time you face a fear, *How is the Lord looking at this right now? Is He upset, worried, uncertain about what to do? Or does He have everything in control and know exactly how He is going to solve this problem?* When we fix our eyes on the Lord and learn to see things from His perspective, we will find that our fears are not based upon anything but the Enemy's desire to keep us in bondage and steal from us the joy of our salvation. Remember who your God is and who you are in Christ the next time fear tries to pull you into its trap. Learn to limit fear. Use it to your advantage to reinforce your commitment to and trust in the Lord. Then you will be able to walk in faith.

Thought #7 — "I must constantly rely on myself if I am ever to get ahead." Our society thrives on independence. The ideal American is self-reliant, a self-starter, and a person who looks out for "number one." Too many Christians start their race well by asking God to show them what He wants done but, in essence, then say, "Thank You, very much. I'll take it from here." They try to work out His plans in their own strength. They have bought into the lie that a person is not worth anything to God unless he or she can accomplish things for Him without the help of others— including the help of God.

When this attitude is present, it is no wonder the Rat Race becomes overwhelming. Too often people will end up running out of steam and exhausted as they try to do by themselves what only God can fully accomplish. Instead of being a conduit, with God's strength and power flowing through them to accomplish His assignments, people drain themselves through self-effort. In fact, their own self-effort can and usually does block the free flow of God's power through them, in much the same way as rocks in a water pipe will slow down the even flow of the pure water.

As with so many things in the Christian life, what we usually see as strength, God sees as weakness. Paul expressed it this way: "For when I am weak, then I am strong" (2 Cor. 12:10). How can this be? It is simple, yet ever so hard to put into practice, especially if you have a lot of talent and abilities. God's ideal is for you to be a servant, to be strong through weakness by letting His Spirit, rather than your own strength be the vehicle of accomplishing through you the good works He has established for you to do.

One of the keys to doing this successfully is to simply acknowledge your total dependence on the Lord for everything from the wisdom to know-how to do something, to the need to have His help in being able to accomplish what it is He is showing you to do. Then, as He offers His help, draw on it by asking for it and consciously choosing to do what He is showing you to do, even though it may seem inconvenient or goes against what you are wanting at the moment.

The bottom line is this: We can run our race in our own strength which is imperfect and often fails us, or instead, we can choose to draw on His perfect strength to live every moment of our lives. When we draw on God's strength, then our limits become our strengths because He supplies His power to meet our weaknesses. As part of this, we need to bring our wrong thoughts under His control (2 Cor. 10:3–5). Many wrong thoughts have some of the same weaknesses and needs. Learning our limits requires that we recognize them.

TRAINING FOR THE RACE

Let's approach this subject from a different angle—that of sports. As I've thought about the Rat Race and the Royal Road, I've noticed some close parallels with different kinds of athletic runners. Each runner has strengths and limits, depending on the type of race. But above all, each needs a trainer—preferably one who has already participated in the very type of competition the runner is going to face.

Successful runners share these qualities:

1. A *desire* to compete and do their best.
2. *Confidence* in themselves to be able to run a good race, do their best, and finish.
3. *Faith* that their trainer will guide them correctly.
4. Willing *submission* to the authority and guidance of their trainer.
5. *Persistence.*
6. A *commitment* to push through the obstacles of pain, strict diet, lack of sleep, and long hours of practice.
7. A *disciplined*, focused life that includes eating and exercising properly
8. *Contentment.*
9. *Integrity.*
10. *Good sportsmanship.*

God has not given each person the same race to compete in. The interesting thing is that God has set it up so everyone who enters can win. You are competing against yourself, against the standards God has determined you are to meet. He wants you to use all of the talent He has given you, and to do it under His direction. If you do so, you are a winner. If you don't, you may finish the race but not receive the prize. Paul talks about this when he says in Galatians 2:2 that he wanted to be certain he had not been "running or had run my race in vain." He knew that the wrong motives or failing to follow God's leading could disqualify him from some of the wonderful things that were available to him in heaven after having run a winning race here on earth.

Some people may say, "I don't want to run a race. I'm happy just being a spectator." But we do not have that option. We are all in a race. The question is which one? We cannot be laid back or lazy because our Trainer is with us to encourage us not only to run, but to run well. Because of God's help and His working in and through us to accomplish His good will, we can have the confidence that He will help us run a good race and finish well.

It will be up to us to do our best with His help. This is where the exercise of time in prayer and feeding on the Word will be essential. No good athlete starts the day without the most nutritious, healthy food he can get, nor does he maintain body tone without special exercises. For the Christian, prayer and proper spiritual nutrition received from reading God's Word are essentials elements. In fact, there is a dual role played by the Word of God. It is both our source of spiritual food and the instruction manual written by our Trainer. It is not enough just to have the actual exercise of the race. The main exercise comes in preparation for the racing event.

Trust and faith in God, our Trainer, and submission to His guidance are essential to be able to run the race well. Persistence in running our race, a commitment to trust the Lord for overcoming all obstacles along the way, and living a disciplined and focused life are essential if we are to finish the race without losing the reward of our prize. God wants us to run our race with joy, not complaining. This doesn't mean that we won't have a discussion with our Trainer on how things are going or have questions about some of His instructions. But it does mean that we will accept His guidance and do the things He asks without complaining and murmuring. When dissatisfaction is allowed to creep in, then the runner will not be able to perform at his best and will fall short of the standard that has been established to win the race.

There will come those times when the runner's body will scream at him to stop or at least slow down. This is the point at which his good training will come in. He will push through that obstacle and get his "second wind." In life, we all have such obstacles and cannot give in to the temptation to give up, compromise, or slow down.

A Race for Each of Us

As in sports, so in the race of life there are different types of runners and different types of races.

Sprinters have hard, fast-paced races. In life, the business types and the mothers of young children best parallel this runner. They have to start their race as fast as they can and never slow down. To win they must stay focused and be at the peak of their performance at all times. When they do slow down, they create great pressures on themselves because they get so far behind. Burnout is not uncommon for this type of "life-sprinter." The race they are in requires that they run at full speed most of the time.

Life-sprinters fortunately are not involved twenty-four hours a day in a full-blown race. They have less intense periods between the times of all-out effort. For the wise sprinter, the periods between the actual races are times of refreshing and preparation for the next leg of race. That can be time spent in earnest with the Lord in the morning before the "race" begins. During the race, remembering all the pertinent instructions of the trainer can help the sprinters adjust their focus and increase their confidence when things may seem impossible.

Middle-distance runners must pace themselves so they have something left to give in the final burst at the end of the race. The married person and those in church leadership come to mind. There is a need to cooperate well with other persons in order to succeed in your own race. You race as a team, not as an individual. Your performance affects that of others. You cannot run a relay alone. You must learn how to pass off to another and let that person carry the burden for a while. However, unlike the sporting event, the one in life's relay keeps on running even though it may not be at the same all out pace that it was before passing the baton. Much of the time in life's race, all teammates are running together in different lanes, but with various paces and responsibilities.

Marathon runners have a hard, long course ahead of them. They need to pace themselves accurately if they are to finish well. They understand their limits and do not go full blast at first. They will have the obstacles of pain, discouragement, and oppression, and, as their bodies tire, will want to shut down. They must keep their eyes on the goal, do the things they have been trained to do in order to get their "second wind." It takes a special runner to run a marathon. Intensive training is to complete the twenty-six plus miles of the course. Without real focus on the goal, a racer will not be able to finish. The marathon runner reminds me of Paul's words at the end of his life: "I have fought the good fight, I have finished the race, I have kept the faith" (2 Tim. 4:7).

Often times marathon runners will have another racer with them who is called the "pace setter." The pace setter's responsibility is to assist the runner by setting a good pace to help the marathon racer finish. Mentors, teachers, pastors, and even parents are "life-pace setters." These people have learned how to run well themselves, and they can help others in their race.

Our fifth runner is the hurdler. Their courses have many obstacles, all of which they are expected to clear. They cannot let any obstacle interfere in their race towards the goal line. Such people can be the single parent, the unemployed, or health-challenged individual. It takes great discipline and coordination to navigate successfully the many barriers between yourself and the ultimate finish line. But with God's help and training it can be done. Sometimes He even helps you by giving you extra strength to get over a specific obstacle.

All runners—and therefore all believers—need to remember that our Trainer, God the Father, is kind. He gives us all we need to compete in whatever race He puts us in. There are no conditions to the promise that says, "I can do all things through Christ who strengthens me" (Phil. 4:13, NKJV) Now obviously, this does not mean a person can fly by himself or swim across the ocean. We were not designed to do so. But it does mean that whatever your Trainer has asked of you, He has equipped you to do, no matter what type of runner you are. It is because of His goodness that He has designed a course on which you can win. And the great thing about it is, that He will be there in the race with you, always encouraging you, guiding you, and helping you do your best.

THE TRAINER

A trainer is the one who knows the ropes, who is able to equip us to be a winner. God is our skilled Trainer. He, in the person of Jesus Christ, has run the race and won. He knows every inch of the course because He has designed it specifically for us. He is kind and good, yet expects the best from us. Unlike a human trainer, He is able to give us the ability to do that which we could never do without Him. He infuses His capabilities and His strengths in us so we will be guaranteed of winning if we follow His game plan or "life map" as we will examine soon in chapter 12. Unlike human runners, God tells us we can do nothing without Him—not even with another trainer.

That other trainer, by the way, is on the sideline. He is the Enemy of our souls. He often tries to trick us into going beyond our limits, of pushing ourselves too far, of trying to run a different race than the one God has for us. He also loves to give us "weights" to carry around with us, making us believe that these extra burdens are part of the race. When we fall into his trap of carrying weights that our Righteous Trainer never meant for us to have, then we are slowed down, and for some even caused to veer off the race onto a detour full of distractions, worries and fears.

Another subtle tactic the false trainer will use is to try to undermine our confidence in either ourselves or our true Trainer. Fortunately for those who were deceived into running The Enemy's race, the one prize of the crown of life can not be taken away. But all other prizes must be won in the right way. So beware of your old trainer. He is not your friend and is working against you as hard as he can.

In the race to win God's prizes, many will start out. Unfortunately, not all will reach their goal. For us believers our aim must be to finish in whichever race God has chosen to put us. We must not try to run another's race. This is part of learning our limits. For some it will be the sprint race, for others it will be the relay or marathon or some other race. May we each run so that we will receive the victor's crown from our Judge, Coach, and Trainer, and see the smile on His face as we cross the line victoriously.

Chapter Seven

Make Better Decisions

In 1210, King John of England had an idea. For many years the Royal Forest was available to all who paid the usage fee. Paying this tribute to the crown allowed nobles and peasants alike to hunt, fish, and frolic on the king's property.

The king, trying to reduce the strain on this resource and to increase the empire's income, decided to raise the fee and restrict the use of the forest to the upper classes. To carry out this decree, he appointed Thomas Mulberry as Royal Forester.

It wasn't long before Thomas realized he had a problem. The king expected a certain amount of revenue each month, but there simply weren't enough customers among the upper classes to maintain the projected revenues.

To keep to the crown's budget, Thomas decided to allow some of the local peasants to use the forest at a discounted rate. This kept the king's coffers filled and, at the same time, still restricted the use of the land to the upper class and a relatively small number of peasants.

After six months, the king summoned Thomas to report. "Well, my Royal Forester, is my plan working as expected?"

"Yes, your Highness," replied Thomas. "Revenues are as projected." The king was obviously pleased.

Added Thomas, "There is one problem, but I made a decision which managed to solve it."

Thomas went on the explain how there were not enough noble-
men to maintain the budgeted revenues and how he allowed some
local peasants to use the land at a discounted rate. The king listened
intently and offered an occasional "Uh-huh," or "Yes, I see."

The following morning Thomas was hanged for treason.[1]

Whether we like it or not, decision making is a vital skill. I realized this
right away as a minister. When I would ask people about their plans for
the future, for the summer, or even next week, I could expect to hear the
phrase, "I don't know."

These words of Dallas Willard aptly describe the quandary many face
when it comes to making decisions.

> Among the loneliest of moments is the time of decision. There the
> weight of our future life clamps down on our hearts. Whatever comes
> will now be our responsibility, 'our fault' . . . . We may find ourselves
> saddled with failures and dreadful consequences that must be carried
> for life.
>
> And soon there follows the time of second thoughts—and third
> and fourth. Did I do the good and wise thing? Is it what God want-
> ed? Is it even what I wanted? Can I live with the consequences? Will
> others think I am a fool? Is God still with me? Will he be with me
> even if it become clear I made the wrong choice? [2]

Many people are caught in the Rat Race because of their inability to make
decisions and follow through on their commitments. Part of the problem
lies in the fact that most people do not fully understand what real decisions
are. In a simple, yet concise form, a real decision is a free, unconditional, and
total commitment to a choice or option. That doesn't mean you cannot
change your mind. Don't see this as a prescription for not collecting the
necessary data to make appropriate decisions. It is simply a choice not to
spend the rest of your week, month, or life second guessing yourself.

Most of us have had to deal with attitudes and roadblocks to the decision-making process. Before I offer you a plan of attack to get on the right
track for making decisions, let's first identify those things which have
proven themselves to be "decision busters."

DECISION BUSTERS

Ours is a fast-paced world. Schedules overlap, commitments conflict,
and a variety of internal and external influences threaten the decision

making process. These influences or "decision busters" almost never exist separately. They all too often operate together and feed upon each other. By neutralizing one of them, it becomes easier to tackle subsequent ones, because we loosen their corporate stronghold upon us. In some cases it is like a domino effect. If you can identify and intercept the primary decision buster and remove it, then the others will also fall.

As with any emotional or physical difficulty, diagnosis is the key. When we are able to recognize and understand the decision busters, we've taken a major step toward victory. As we know from the spiritual dimension, it is almost impossible to fight against an unseen, or even worse—an unknown—enemy. This is why Scripture emphasizes our need to put on the armor of God and not be unaware of Satan's schemes. The more we understand, the better equipped we will be in warfare.

We will now look at some of the most common and powerful decision busters that impact our lives. These busters are not arranged in order of importance; they are all destructive. This list is not all-inclusive either. I am sure we could easily describe other specific blockages, but most of them would probably be derived from these major ones.

Fear of Change

Most people prefer the status quo. The known enemy is less threatening than the unknown friend. We want new benefits but often are afraid of the steps it takes to secure them. Unreasonable fear intimidates and holds many a person captive to the Rat Race. It does not allow them to take the necessary steps to get out of the mess they are in.

To many people, decision making represents a pending change and unwanted stress. So their response is a subtle attempt to put a barrier between themselves and any possibility of the change. People handle change and subsequent decisions in a variety of ways.

Some resist change. They wrestle with what I call a hardening of the attitudes. And, of course, it is foolish to resist change because change is going to happen whether we like it or not. If you don't believe me, take a long look at your high school graduation picture. Things change! It's like the two caterpillars who were talking to each other on the ground They both looked up and saw a butterfly and one said to the other, "You'd never get me up in one of those things."

Sometimes we react to change. People may not be that happy with the status quo, but then neither are they pleased with change. I saw this in

Jeff's face as he and his wife sat in my office. As we talked about fears that were shutting him down emotionally, it became apparent that one source of these fears was his job. He had been there ten years and was intimidated by his bosses. The poor economic climate in California had given management a tool to hold over their employees' heads: Don't complain, or you may end up without a job. Jeff hated the pressure, couldn't sleep well, was grouchy, and reacted negatively anytime his wife suggested looking for a new job. He resented her interference yet couldn't continue living as he was. He had allowed his reactions to change to keep him bound to a job that was unhealthy for him. Fortunately, once he realized this, he was able to start looking for a new job, trusting the Lord to give him one that would be right for him.

Pastors see similar problems all of the time. We know from experience that certain changes in the church services will attract more people to our church. But often the older members resist such changes. They know things are not going well, yet they also know they don't want to see innovations put in if it means any changes in what they currently are doing. Just try changing the music of the traditional service—even if it is only introducing words projected on the wall or screen. You will find people who will resist, even to the point of considering leaving the church. In one church I pastored, a couple left the church when the room for their Sunday School class was changed. People often react to change without reasonable justification.

Lastly, many people run from change and thus from making decisions. This is one step further than resisting, because when we run, we are not even considering the alternatives. We have decided nothing should change, so nothing is an acceptable proposal. We surround ourselves with our memories and previous successes and by doing so, we alienate ourselves from the present and the future. The older we get, the more we want security, and anything that shakes our comfortable nest threatens us. We then become afraid to make a necessary decision for fear of the possible repercussions. Running away is the ultimate way out. So people will leave their children, change their jobs, or move to another area. But running from the pain or the change does not remove it.

Resignation

While some people will withdraw and hide, others cling tenaciously to things as they are. Resignation begins with an attempt to avert pain and internal conflict by avoiding emotional investment. They see options and choices as having the potential to tear apart their lives and produce tremendous anxiety. The status quo seems to be the only safe harbor.

This detachment creates difficulty in relationships as well. Friends, mates, and even children are frustrated by a resigned individual's apparent indifference and coldness. Oftentimes, all that the resigned person needs is a little motivation. Sometimes, all a person needs is to be challenged with a doable vision for progress. Sadly, though, it sometimes takes a tragedy, such as a death or a loss of a job, to spur people to change.

Confusion

Not knowing our priorities is a major decision buster. If we would admit it, most of us are not even aware that we have fallen victims to this roadblock.

Our priorities will determine how we spend our time and energy. Scott and Vickie Wilson, who have been dear friends of my family for many years, place a high priority on family time together. Scott is in law enforcement and found that the hectic pace of city life was imposing on his time with his wife and four sons. So he said, "Good-bye, city life," (sounds a little like "Green Acres" doesn't it?) and moved to a remote area in the mountains where he built a home for his family. Scott did not do this because of his desire to withdraw or his inability to make friends, but because his priorities were clear. His commitment to spend time with his family made the decision to move an easy one.

Learning your priorities may take a lifetime. But remember, each time you refrain from making a decision, you virtually declare yourself to be priority-free, allowing a vicious cycle of indecisiveness to feed upon itself.

Depression

It is difficult to function in any area of life when we feel hopeless. Depression is a major "decision buster" because it is always accompanied by anxiety.

Dr. Gary Collins shares, "Depression (or melancholia, as it was once known) has been recognized as a common problem for more than 2000 years. Recently, however, it has come so much into public attention that some are calling our era the 'age of melancholy,' in contrast to the 'age of anxiety' which followed World War II." He adds, "The signs of depression include sadness, apathy and inertia which make it difficult to 'get along' or make decisions." [3]

The Rat Race can be depressing. We place extremely high expectations upon ourselves. Success and achievement are wonderful, but they will never provide eternal health, endless life, or guaranteed joy.

There are many telltale warning signs of depression. The most telling signs include a person's inability to make effective decisions despite valiant efforts and a desire to escape from pressures. It is as though his decision-making abilities were caught in molasses, slowing down his thought process, and eventually leading to the person's avoiding any significant decision. If depression is your decision buster, it may be time to consider seeking counseling.

Pride

One of the more intense decision busters is *pride*. It comes in many packages. The executive manager who gets laid off in the reorganization of a company may find it difficult to take a taxi driving job or that of a janitor —not only because of the financial considerations, but because of pride. He views himself to be in a much higher position and may find it difficult to do the expedient in order to meet his family's needs.

Pride also can interfere in the decision of older people to cut back in their style of living when retirement draws near: getting a more economical car, moving to a small home or condo, giving up some of the luxury vacations, and dining out less often. These can all be difficult situations and can become decision busters if the person has not learned to regard possessions and reputation lightly.

Walking the fine line between pride and humility can be like walking a tightrope. On one side you fall down and you feel like you're depriving yourself, and the other side you fall down and you become haughty.

Subordination

One form of defensive strategy with which some people use to cope is to transfer decision making to someone else and to become dependent upon that someone's input and advice. People who become overly dependent upon other people's tastes, opinions, and decisions often reach a point where they never consult themselves.

This form of codependency can be crippling, yet dependency of this type is common. Drs. Hemfelt, Minirth, Meier, Newman, and Newman have outlined twenty-one statements that help clarify this kind of behavior. See if this list describes you.

1. _____ I can't stand to be alone.
2. _____ I am a perfectionist.
3. _____ I am driven by the approval of others.
4. _____ I feel desperate when I cannot gain the approval of other people.
5. _____ I find myself making decisions based on how they will affect other people and rarely consider myself.
6. _____ Many times I feel obsessed by a need for total order in my life.
7. _____ I put work first, above anything.
8. _____ I find myself adjusting to my spouse's needs rather than communicating my feelings.
9. _____ I do not experience anger.
10. _____ I overeat often.
11. _____ I am constantly wondering what other people think of me.
12. _____ I cover up my feelings so others won't realize what I really think.
13. _____ I am afraid that if others really knew me they would run and hide.
14. _____ I am constantly trying to figure how to stay ahead in my relationships.
15. _____ I cover up my feelings of self-doubt with drug or alcohol use.
16. _____ I can't say no when I am asked to do a favor or serve on a committee.
17. _____ When I begin to feel sad or angry I go shopping, work harder, or eat.
18. _____ I tell myself it shouldn't hurt so much when others let me down.
19. _____ I need to control those close to me.
20. _____ I need everyone to be happy with me so that I can feel good about myself.
21. _____ I need others to be strong for me without requiring anything from me in return.[4]

Their conclusion is that if just two of these statements are checked as appropriate for you, you may have codependent or subordinate issues worth exploring. You see, none of us has all the facts, none of us is an expert in everything, but to become consistently dependent upon others is a "decision buster."

Important Principles in Decision Making

Decision making is an unavoidable part of life. Some of the decisions you will make are trivial. "What program should I watch on television?" "Where do you want to go to lunch after church today?" Some of the decisions are major. "Will I marry?" "Should we have children?" But not to make a decision is to be trapped in the vise of indecision.

Have you ever noticed that some people seem to have an easier time making decisions than others? If they make a mistake, their world doesn't fall apart. They would rather do something wrong than to do nothing at all. Other people have trouble looking at a menu and choosing what they want to eat for one meal. These are the ones who get caught in the Rat Race of indecisiveness.

Because we are human beings, we have a great potential for error. We wait too long; we pay too much; and we will make wrong decisions. In order for us to enjoy life the way God intended, we need to examine some of the principles outlined in Scripture for decision making. There is no clear cut formula in the Bible because there are so many different types of decisions. But God gives us distinct principles that can make the decision making process much simpler.

Principle #1 — Request wisdom from God. I have found that when people face confusion in their lives, they react in one of three ways. They may panic. They are not sure which way to turn or which choice to make. Life becomes a series of anxiety attacks. Some people will ponder. Many find relief in never making a decision. They do not want to face life, they just want to think about it. These are the people who hope the problem will just go away. A third option is to pray. James, the brother of the Lord Jesus Christ, wrote, "If any of you lacks wisdom, he should ask God, who gives generously to all without finding fault, and it will be given to him" (James 1:5). God Himself tells us that the wisest thing we can do is to ask Him for wisdom.

I have the wonderful opportunity of traveling throughout the United States speaking on the topics leadership, evangelism, assimilation, and the process of change in the church. I also accept opportunities to go into a church as a consultant, diagnosing the problems that are hindering a church from reaching its potential and establishing a plan both to encourage and motivate the church body. These churches are relying upon my expertise and experience to help them make a decision. Ultimately, through every believer has God as a consultant. And it is comforting to know and claim the promise that though I may be confused, God is not. He never gets tired of helping us. He has never said or will ever say, "Don't bother me, I can't believe you've got another problem." God is always waiting for us to ask. We are told in Proverbs 2:6, "For the Lord gives wisdom, and from his mouth come knowledge and understanding."

Suppose God came to you one day and asked you what you would like or want more than anything else. What would you ask for? In the Old Testament, Solomon had such an opportunity. God came to him and said, "Solomon, you're the King of Israel and I'm going to grant you one wish. What do you want more than anything else in life?" Solomon must have thought it over and said, "God, I'm so inadequate as a leader. I don't know what to do with these people. God, more than anything else, I want wisdom. I want to be able to think like You think. I want to be able to see things from Your point of view. I want the ability to make decisions the way You would make them. I don't want to look back on my life and have regrets. I want wisdom." And the Bible records that God was pleased with Solomon's request and granted it (1 Kings 3:5–12). If you had been given this one chance in a lifetime, what would you have wished for? Whatever it is that tops your list, wisdom is more important.

Principle #2 — Rely on God's provision. In James 1, we read, "But when he asks, he must believe and not doubt. . . ." In other words, expect an answer. Trust that God did hear your request, now rely on His provision.

It appears in the decision making process that first we must ask the right person—God—then we must ask in the right way—in faith, believing and not doubting. All of us have prayed for something and then said, "I knew I'd never get it." "I've been praying for a job change, but I doubt if it will ever become a reality." "I prayed for a mate, but I'm getting up in years and realize that the chances are slim."

Don't confuse faith with presumption. Presumption says, "I believe that God will make this decision for me." Faith says, "Lord I believe that you will give me the wisdom to make this decision." Decision making is one way God molds us and makes us more like Jesus Christ. If, as a parent, I made every decision for my children, what kind of adults would they grow up to be? They would be totally dependent and they would lack maturity. Have you ever seen a child who is so smothered by his parents that he is afraid of the world? What indecisiveness produces is fear. Is there a time to wait on the Lord? Of course there is. But there is also a time to rely on the belief that God will help direct what He wants me to do.

Doubt can be debilitating. Remember Peter? He was in a boat one day with the other disciples and Jesus was heading toward the boat, walking on the water. Peter said to himself, "Great idea," and he jumped out of the boat and started walking to the Lord. Peter had his eyes on the Lord, and he was doing fine. Then he took his eyes off of Jesus and looked at where he was. He probably thought to himself, *I can't do this. How did I get myself into this?* What happened? He began to sink.

Our steps of faith are pleasing to God: "Without faith it is impossible to please God, because anyone who comes to him must believe that he exists and that he rewards those who earnestly seek him" (Heb. 11:6). Evidently, if you are to receive anything from God, you have to believe in advance that you are going to get it. That's faith!

Principle #3 — Rest in Your Decision. James moves us beyond doubt, saying, "But when he asks, he must believe and not doubt, because he who doubts is like a wave of the sea, blown and tossed by the wind. That man should not think he will receive anything from the Lord; he is a double-minded man, unstable in all he does" (James 1:6–7). In other words, we should not second-guess ourselves, realizing that no man who puts his hand to the plow and looks back is fit for the kingdom of heaven.

Have you ever tried to straddle a fence? I bet you didn't do it for long, because it gets very uncomfortable. *Whenever you try to carry two decisions or two options around with you for any length of time, the stress of the Rat Race becomes even more apparent in three areas of instability.*

First, there is emotional instability. You spend more time worrying and stewing instead of doing. Constantly you ask youself, *Did I do the right thing? Did I make the right choice?* Indecisiveness has a predictable pattern. Instability in your emotional life leaves you confused, unable to think, often unable to eat and thoroughly miserable.

Second, there is relational instability. Anytime a person is indecisive about a relationship, there will also be a lack of commitment. This lack of commitment is seen as a person attempts to decide whether to leave or stay. It may be a career decision in which you change from job to job, searching for the ideal place. It may be a mother who says one thing to her child but changes her mind for no apparent reason, sending mixed messages to her son or daughter. I have personally found that far more energy is expended in *deciding* than in *doing*. And until the doing takes place in a relationship, there is instability.

The third and final area of instability is spiritual instability. James 1:7 states, "That man should not think he will receive anything from the Lord . . . ." Indecisiveness blocks your prayers and keeps you from receiving what God has to offer. This indecision is evident when we attempt to do our own will and God's will at the same time. It is inevitable that double-mindedness will produce a double life. This person could sing "Onward Christian Soldiers" on Sunday and go AWOL on Monday.

Figure 7–1

Principle #4 — Relate to the facts, not your feelings. Why do we waver? Why do we doubt? One of the main reasons is because we focus on our feelings and not on the facts. Feelings are not stable. Those who make decisions that are based purely on emotion find themselves doubting the wisdom of their decision. This is why when I speak with an unbeliever about receiving Christ, I will not try to work up a lot of emotion. I see evangelists who rely upon emotions to stir the audience to make decisions, and I have found that such decisions last just about as long as the emotions last.

Feelings are a major part of life. We need them, but we cannot always rely on them. The best piece of advice I have ever received goes like this: *Never make a major decision when you are tired, depressed, sick, or emotionally stressed.* As a pastor, I will never make a major decision on Monday. If pastors lived their lives solely on emotions, most of us would resign on Monday. It is hard to be logical when you are emotionally spent or upset. So you shouldn't walk out of your marriage when you're depressed. You should never change jobs because your boss is angry with you. You must first look at the emotions and examine the facts. Ask God, then make the decision.

Principle #5 — Re-establish your life on the Bible. James 1:22–25 reminds us, "Do not merely listen to the word, and so deceive yourselves. Do what it says. Anyone who listens to the word but does not do what it says is like a man who looks at his face in a mirror and, after looking at himself, goes away and immediately forgets what he looks like. But the man who looks intently into the perfect law that gives freedom, and continues to do this, not forgetting what he has heard, but doing it—he will be blessed in what he does."

Do you really want the wisdom of God in your life? Then you will need the word of God in your heart. I hear people say all the time, "I asked for wisdom to make this decision, and I didn't get it." What I would ask these people is, "How often do you read your Bible?" I have discovered two important guidelines concerning God's will for our lives. First God's will is found in God's Word. If you are not reading your Bible, you will not discover God's will for your life. Second, God's will is never contrary to God's Word. Many have asked, "How can it be so wrong, when it feels so right?" I'll tell you why. Feelings are unreliable. It's not enough to go to church on Sunday, anticipating that you will receive enough spiritual nourishment for the remainder of the week. You will forget the majority of what you hear anyway. How can we retain what we hear?

James 1:22–25 provides three tools we can use to hold onto God's word longer and thus provide a firmer foundation for the decision making process.

- *Study the Bible* — By the one who "looks intently into the perfect law." Get into a Bible study, join a small group, do whatever it takes to get into the Bible and get it into you.
- *Memorize the Bible* — No, not the entire Bible, but portions of it which will revolutionize your life. Be the one who continues to do this, "not forgetting what he has heard."
- *Do what you learn in the Bible* — Be the one who *does* what he hears—"he will be blessed in what he does." Follow the Bible, put it into practice, and trust that it will truly change your life. Stability is found in knowing God's Word. "It was He who gave some to be apostles, some to be prophets, some to be evangelists, and some to be pastors and teachers, to prepare God's people for works of service, so that the body of Christ may be built up until we all reach unity in the faith and in the knowledge of the Son of God and become mature, attaining to the whole measure of the fullness of Christ. Then we will no longer be infants, tossed back and forth by the waves, and blown here and there by every wind of teaching" (Eph. 4:11–14a). The more you base your life on the Bible, the more stable you become.

Making decisions is an important part of climbing out of the Rat Race and back into God's Royal Race. He will not make all of your decisions for you. He has given us the freedom to decide. He does, however, desire your decisions be based upon His wisdom. We are told in Psalm 119:105 that "Your [God's] word is a lamp to my feet and a light for my path." In Jesus' day, they didn't have flashlights with batteries that keep on going and going. So how did the people walk in the dark? They had tiny lamps that would not allow the oil to slosh out. They would light the lamps, and then strap them to the front of their shoes. And as they took each step, the light would shine just far enough ahead so they would be able to keep walking. The Bible is this kind of light. It is not a high beam that shows us everything that will happen up ahead over the next ten years. God doesn't want us looking that far ahead because we'd panic. He wants us to live one day at a time. One decision at a time. And He has promised to give us the wisdom necessary for each step we take. Once we know how to make decisions, we are ready to look at God's method for breaking the cycle of busyness. To do so is a wise decision.

Chapter Eight

Break the Cycle of Busyness

Busy Man

Lord, forgive me—
I've failed You again.

Some believers wouldn't consider it a failure,
but I know better.

It's not prayerlessness, not this time.
Nor evil thoughts or vain imagination.
Or even unholy ambition.

No, I've failed You in a much more subtle way.
I've become the ugliest of all things—a busy man.

It was okay for a while.
The long hours,

the constant pressure—
   reports to make, people to see
       unrealistic expectations, relentless
           demands. . . .

I loved what I was doing.
I was committed,
   creative,
       energetic. . . .
Like a quick change artist
I switched hats,
changed roles,
   tried to be all things to all people.

There was no time for solitude or daydreaming,
People always talking to me,
   materials to prepare,
       deadlines to meet.

It was exciting and demanding.
I was out to change the world.
But there was no rhythm to my life,
no balance between work and rest, worship and play.

Now I'm not just a busy man.
I'm an angry man too.
I'm tempted to resent the people I love
and to dread the work I'm committed to.

Forgive me, Lord,
for working too hard and playing far too little.
Let me become a child again
at least for a time each day.

Balance my busyness with solitude,
my work with rest.
Let me walk away from time to time
so I can return refreshed and renewed.

Help me Lord, for I am a busy man.[1]

Time is life. You cannot replace it, and you'll never reverse it. To waste your time is to waste your life, but when and if you can master your time, you will make the most of your life. Some people mistake hurrying for managing their time. They try to do more and be more. They expect others to do more and be more. When their expectations aren't met, they become impatient. Impatience is the third warning sign of being caught in the Rat Race. So let's look at the relationship between time, impatience, and hurrying.

Life in the Rat Race is a matter of time out of control. When we bring our time under control by using it properly, then we no longer have to hurry or become impatient. Since no synonym can do justice to everything I mean by control, let me illustrate with a couple I'll call Tim and Beth. They're not a "real" couple, but we all know people like them. They led storybook lives, seemingly having it all, yet really only having everyone fooled. They enjoyed vigorous health and good looks, wonderful children, successful careers, but one day they awakened to the reality that they had no time to talk. Every second counted. They hit the floor running—kids to get ready for school, lunches to make, a last-minute homework assignment to check, car-pooling duties for half the neighborhood, and finally, on to their respected jobs. They seemed locked into their morning schedule. The more they hurried, the less time there seemed to be. Their nerves got frazzled as they felt the mounting pressure of the fast paced life. They often let impatience rule as they succumbed to these pressures with the resulting emotional fallout.

So when could they find a little peace and quiet, some relief from the pressures and mounting impatience? In the evening when they got home? No, then there was dinner to prepare, repairs to do, groceries to put away, homework to help with, phone calls to make, bank books to balance (or bills to pay, or dogs to walk, or letters to write, or kids to take to a meeting or sporting practice), picking up the mess of the last twenty-four hours, checking the answering machine, making more phone calls, and so it went. And for much of the evening their bodies cried out "STOP!" but who could stop with so much still left to do?

Fifteen hours after getting up their heads hit their pillows. Their exhausted minds asked, *Where has the fun gone? How has this happened to us?* Worse than that, they feel pressured all the time, like being on a merry-go-round that seems to be whirling faster and faster until it makes them feel so dizzy that they're afraid to jump off. They have been caught in a time trap and they, like many, have no idea how to escape it.

TIME CONTROLLERS

In an effort to take control of a scenario like Tom's and Beth's, some people overcompensate when it comes to time control. Believe it or not, your efforts to manage time can wind up taking control of your life. Check yourself to make sure you're not caught in one of these traps.

The Time Analyzer

The time analyzer lives and dies making lists, updating lists, losing lists, and comparing lists. When you approach him about doing something, he tends to spend much more time contemplating the possibilities and planning the details than doing anything. If he knows that everything is planned, he feels organized. Will he get anything *done* today? Probably not—but there is always tomorrow's list. He finds himself blind to change, oblivious to new opportunities, and unaware of the needs of people around him.

The Time Condenser

The time condenser is so busy trying to accomplish and attain that he finds little time to assess the true value of what he is working for. I have found these people to be somewhat unapproachable because they have a tendency to want to tell everyone else what to do. They are inflexible and terribly efficient. They also sometimes discover that the ladder on which they were climbing to success was leaning on the wrong building.

The Time Fanatic

The time fanatic is preoccupied with time. Everyone around him is on edge because "time is money." He is the one with an impossible schedule. You have often asked such people, "How do you get it all done?" They answer, "You just have to use your time to the fullest." They will never start a meeting late, will always keep careful records with great detail of what needs to be done every day. They know how to save time in every area of their lives, from laying out their clothes the night before to eating their breakfast in the car on the way to work.

Now, don't get me wrong. Each of the three has potentially valuable traits, but carried to the extreme, these traits become liabilities. No one type is better off than the other two. It is just as bad to be totally disorganized as it is to be overly organized and going through life at a frenetic pace—the pace of the Rat Race.

USING TIME WISELY

Time that is lost can never be found again. There are no time savings accounts, no time lay-away plans. Time can be wasted but never recycled. And there just never seems to be enough of this precious commodity to get everything done that you would like to. Too often I feel like an Egyptian mummy—pressed for time.

In my life, there are many people I have personally chosen as models. I want to be an encourager like Neil Anderson. Neil, who has written numerous books on being free in Christ (*The Bondage Breaker,* Harvest House 1990; *Victory Over Darkness,* Gospel Light, 1990), was a great encouragement to me while attending seminary. His transparent heart, love for the Lord, and ability to sense the good in every situation still motivates me in the ministry.

I want to have the compassion for the Lord's work and people like Gary McIntosh. Gary and I have written two books together, and I treasure his expertise, but more importantly treasure his love for his family and mine. I remember Gary telling me what he wanted written on his tombstone, "He loved the Lord, he loved his wife, and he loved his sons."

I want to have the focus and the wise use of my life as did the apostle Paul. Paul wrote to a church in Ephesus from his prison cell in Rome. Despite his circumstances, he had never lost the wonder of what God had done in and through his life. He knew, as we do, that we owe an eternal thanks to God for His marvelous salvation. And in this letter, he wasted no time in raising the subjects of grace, mercy, and God's kindness to him.

Paul gives us a glimpse into his wise use of time. He shares in Ephesians 5:15 (NASB) "Therefore be careful how you walk, not as unwise men, but as wise . . ." Paul tells us that we need to be careful how we live. Is this a reference to freeway driving? Could Paul be emphasizing the need for family time? I'm convinced that verse sixteen gives us an insight: "making the most of your time, because the days are evil." The context appears to be one of taking meticulous care in engineering our spiritual priorities. In our careers, we know that careful planning prevents inefficiency and waste. We must do the same in our spiritual lives, to be wise with the time that God has given us. The word *evil* in verse sixteen has the idea of something painful or laborious. In our terminology, life is a hassle! So what's the answer? We need to manage our time wisely, and Paul gives us four principles that are vital to successfully controlling our time.

Evaluate Your Activities

What Paul says in verse fifteen, "Therefore be careful how you walk, not as unwise men, but as wise," represents a call to look carefully into your life and become aware of where all of your time is going. I wonder how many times I have heard someone say, "I wonder where all the time went?" You will never be able to answer this question without evaluating what you are doing with your time.

An average seventy-year-old man has spent twenty-four years sleeping, fourteen years working, eight years in amusements, six years at the dinner table, five years in transportation, four years in conversation, three years in education, and two years in studying and reading.

His other four years were spent in miscellaneous pursuits. Of those four years, he spent forty-five minutes in church on Sundays, and five minutes were devoted to prayer each day. This adds up to a not at all impressive total of five months that he gave to God over the seventy years of his life.[2]

You read statistics like these and hope they aren't true . . . but they are. Most people are carelessly giving away large chunks of life. A healthy assignment that I have given my staff is to keep a log of their activities for an entire week. After this tedious chore is finished, I challenge them to evaluate where they have been putting their time. They are encouraged to ask themselves some extremely penetrating questions:

- Am I satisfied with my priorities?
- Where will I be five years from now if this continues to be my weekly schedule?
- What is my aim? What are my goals?
- Is there a need to reprioritize my efforts or reevaluate my schedule?

Operate in the Present

Notice Paul's declaration in Ephesians 5:16, "making the most of your time, because the days are evil." We are called to make the very best use of our time and to capitalize on present opportunities, or they will slip away.

How would you respond if someone came up to you offering you a bank account so fully stocked that every day you had to spend $86,400? You didn't have to do a thing, just spend that much money every day of every week of every year. What would you do with it? I'm sure there are a myriad of things you could and would do, but you sure wouldn't waste it by leaving it in the account. First thing every morning, there you'd be at the automatic teller machine withdrawing your $86,400 looking forward to a great day of shopping.

Every day, you are given 86,400 golden seconds to use. And guess what—if you don't use them, you will definitely lose them. Remember once again, time can be wasted, but it can never be recycled. So here is a very simple piece of advice: *Don't procrastinate!* This concept is biblical.

- "Do not boast about tomorrow, for you do not know what a day may bring forth" (Prov. 27:1).
- "Come now, you who say, 'Today or tomorrow, we shall go to such and such a city, and spend a year there and engage in business and make a profit.' Yet you do not know what your life will be like tomorrow. You are just a vapor that appears for a little while and then vanishes away. Instead, you ought to say, 'If the Lord wills, we shall live and also do this or that.' But as it is, you boast in your arrogance; all such boasting is evil" (James 4:13–16, NASB).
- "And let us not lose heart in doing good, for in due time we shall reap if we do not grow weary." (Gal. 6:9, NASB).

Haven't you discovered that opportunities never seem to last? Take coupons, for instance. I remember our son, Scott, trying to cash in a pizza coupon that read, "For a limited time only." It was so limited that it had expired, and we had to pay full price. If you don't use it, you will lose it and often suffer loss in the process.

Appreciate What's Important

Follow Paul's thinking as we read in Ephesians 5:17, "So then do not be foolish, but understand what the will of the Lord is." There is no more important place in which to be than in the center of God's will for your life.

Much of life is wasted by pursuing the unimportant. We only have so much time. Let me illustrate. Here is how much time I have in a given day.

Figure 8–1

I can choose to use it anyway I please, with certain limitations (i.e., I need to eat, sleep, and take care of the basic functions of life). Typically, eighty percent of my time is spent in those areas that I will call "urgent." They cry out for time and attention, even though they are not as important in the long run as are my priorities. The other twenty percent is devoted to the priorities of life, including my walk with the Lord, my relationships, and service. So here is how my time and attention diagram would look:

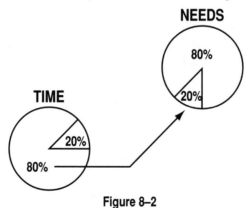

Figure 8–2

Doesn't it make more sense to focus the twenty percent on the twenty percent and to allot only a few hours of each day to those items that are not so that important? We need to place that twenty percent of energy into those urgent twenty percent of the problems and let our priorities have the eighty percent. This would be good stewardship of our time.

You must appreciate what's important. I know people who spend more time with Dan Dierdorf and Al Michaels than they do reading the Bible. I

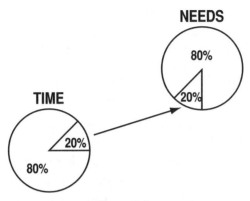

Figure 8–3

know people who know more about their favorite soap stars than they do about Jesus. The typical Sunday newspaper has more words in it than the entire New Testament. Many people have no difficulty wading through this paper every week but have great difficulty reading their Bibles even for a short time.

You need to know what's the most important in life, because God has given you more than enough time to know His will for your life and how to accomplish it. Some of the earliest recorded words of our Lord include these in Luke 2:49 (KJV), "I must be about My Father's business." Then at the end of His life, hanging on a cross for our sins, Scripture records Him saying, "It is finished." What was finished? Everything God the Father had asked Him to do. Had every sick person been healed? No! Had everyone become a disciple or had everyone heard His message? No way! But what the Father wanted done—the redemption of humanity—had been accomplished by His obedient Son.

God's will for your life can be summarized in three words: knowing, growing, and going. God wants you to know Him intimately, to have a personal relationship with Him.

- "For I know the thoughts that I think toward you, says the LORD, thoughts of peace and not of evil, to give you a future and a hope. Then you will call upon me and go and pray to Me, and I will listen to you. And you will seek Me and find Me, when you search for Me with all your heart. I will be found by you, says the LORD" (Jer. 29:11–14, NKJV).
- "Draw near to God and He will draw near to you" (James 4:8a, NASB).

- "I will instruct you and teach you in the way you should go; I will counsel you and watch over you" (Psalm 32:8).
- "The Lord confides in those who fear him . . ." Ps. 25:14.

God also wants you to grow, to mature and develop in your faith. That's why He has given you the Bible and His church.

- "Blessed are they whose ways are blameless, who walk according to the law of the Lord. Blessed are they who keep his statutes and seek him with all their heart. They do nothing wrong; they walk in his ways. You have laid down precepts that are to be fully obeyed. Oh, that my ways were steadfast in obeying your decrees! Then I would not be put to shame when I consider all your commands. I will praise you with an upright heart as I learn your righteous laws. I will obey your decrees; do not utterly forsake me. How can a young man keep his way pure? By living according to your word" (Ps. 119:1–9).

Last, we need to go and tell others about Him and His love for us. God wants us to share our faith and help others to understand what the Lord Jesus Christ came to earth to accomplish.

- "All authority in heaven and on earth has been given to me. Therefore go and make disciples of all nations, baptizing them in the name of the Father and of the Son and of the Holy Spirit, and teaching them to obey everything I have commanded you" (Matt 28:18–20).
- "Don't forget to pray for us, too, that God will give us many chances to preach the Good News of Christ for which I am here in jail. Pray that I will be bold enough to tell it freely and fully, and make it plain, as, of course, I should. Make the most of your chances to tell others the Good News" (Col. 4:3–5, TLB).

These are the basics, the important things, and when you don't have the basics in focus, all the rest of life seems just a little out of balance.

Regulate the Pressure

I do a lot of flying and whenever I get on the plane I hear the same thing, "Ladies and gentlemen, our cabin has been pressurized for your comfort." The way I understand this, (despite the fact that my engineer friends say that I don't fully get it), is that they are putting air into the plane to maintain the fourteen pounds per square inch necessary to keep us comfortable. Whatever the external pressure may be, the internal pressure must be the same or the cabin will collapse.

We are wired in much the same way. Paul writes in Ephesians 5:18, "And do not get drunk with wine, for that is dissipation, but be filled with the Spirit." Whenever the stress and pressure mount, we try to fill our lives with something to regulate the inside. The choice we have is, what to fill ourselves with. Some turn to alcohol, drugs, tranquilizers, or even use smoking as a relaxant. I have always struggled with food. When I am under stress, my idea of a balanced meal is a burger in both hands. Paul in essence says, that we should fill our lives with the Spirit of God and allow God's presence to regulate the pressure.

PUTTING OUR TIME UNDER THE SPIRIT'S CONTROL

Since its inception, Campus Crusade for Christ International has had a strong emphasis on walking in the control of the Holy Spirit moment by moment. In commenting on Romans 7:18b–20, Steve Douglass, their executive vice-president, says, "In the next chapter of Romans, Paul explains that people were never intended to live the Christian life, which is a supernatural life, without a supernatural source of power. If that's true, then what does God expect us to do? Here's the answer: He wants us to let Him live the Christian life in and through us. This means that God's Spirit, the Holy Spirit, supplies everything we need to live the Christian life successfully. He has supernatural power, and He is always available. The key to a joyful walk with God—the absolute necessity—is the Holy Spirit." [3]

Chuck Swindoll does an excellent job in spelling out the heart of the Spirit filled life.

> We become Christians because we receive Christ Jesus the Lord. We become empowered and filled with the Spirit as we "walk in Him." Both are essential if we hope to enjoy all the benefits of the Christian life, for it is possible to be converted and yet not live on a spiritual plane. It is one thing to become a Christian. It is another thing entirely to become a Spirit-filled Christian. The tragedy is that so many are converted and so few Spirit-filled. When this happens, a person misses the best God has to offer us on earth.
>
> What fuel is to a car, the Holy Spirit is to the believer. He energizes us to stay the course. He motivates us in spite of the obstacles. He keeps us going when the road gets rough. It is the Spirit who comforts

us in our distress, who calms us in times of calamity, who becomes our companion in loneliness and grief, who spurs our "intuition" into action, who fills our minds with discernment when we are uneasy about a certain decision. In short, He is our spiritual fuel. When we attempt to operate without Him or to use some substitute fuel, all systems grind to a halt.[4]

He goes on to emphasize the key missing ingredient for those caught in the Rat Race:

Even though every believer has the Holy Spirit, it is possible to operate our lives apart from his control. But when that happens—which it does with many Christians every day—what is missed is nothing short of tragic. When we operate under His control, the potential for peace and joy, calm and comfort, guidance and insight, confidence and courage know no bounds. That is not an exaggeration; it is fact. `This is why an understanding of the filling of the Spirit is absolutely crucial."[5]

But some people don't know how to live under the Spirit's control. Charles Stanley identifies one key reason for this in many people's lives. He believes that it

concerns their early days as Christians. Generally, when people are born again, an excitement about their newfound life manifests itself by way of a whole lot of activity. This is especially true of people who are saved during their teens or later. This burst of spiritual energy makes it thrilling to spend time with new believers. They can't get to church early enough. They can't pray enough. They show up at every Bible study. They witness. They attend seminars. They carry their Bibles everywhere. They are unstoppable. The same is often true of a believer who comes back to the Lord after a prodigal son-type experience.

Well, all of this is fine except for one small detail. The energy source of all their activity is usually their own human strength—which, of course, is being fueled by the genuine joy that accompanies salvation or restoration. Don't misunderstand me. I am in no way criticizing the zeal that accompanies faith in Christ. We would all benefit from spending more time with new Christians. The problem is that they usually assume that what they are experiencing will last forever. If no one instructs them on how to walk in the Spirit, they will continue in their own strength—doing the best they can, which for a while is really pretty good! Eventually, however, they run out of steam. They grow tired of the activity. The emotional high subsides. And they wonder what the problem is. Determined not to regress, they dig in their heels and, you guessed it, do the best they can.[6]

This is part of why we get caught in the Rat Race. We are struggling to live our life in the best way we can. We feel pressures. But instead of giving Him all our burdens and cares, we look for ways *we* can get relief on our own. It is human nature to want to do things in our own strength. Yet Paul tells us that when he is weakest, it is then that he is the strongest. He has learned that it is at such times of weakness that the Holy Spirit will give us His strength flowing through us to meet any and all needs—if we allow Him to. This is the principle that any Christian, but especially one caught in the pressures of the Rat Race, needs to learn.

But I can almost hear some of you asking, "How does one become filled with the Holy Spirit?" If you're a Christian, the Holy Spirit already lives inside of you. Allowing Him to have control of your daily life is a commitment you make every day. First you need to understand that this is something God wants us to do. In Ephesians 5:18, we are told to be "filled with the Spirit." God would not ask us to do something that He does not show us how to do. So we then can take the next step of asking Him to fill us, based on His promise in 1 John 5:14–15 in which we are told that "if we ask anything according to His will, He hears us. And if we know that He hears us in whatever we ask, we know that we have the requests which we have asked from Him." This is a straightforward proposition: Ask of God something that you know is His will, like being filled with the Spirit, and then you can know that He not only hears your request, but will also answer it because what you have asked is already His will.

In practical terms, a person can pray a prayer similar to the following:

Lord Jesus, I have been in control of my life, but I now want Your Spirit to be the One who runs my life. I am giving You all of my rights. Please take control of every area of my life. Whenever I am tempted to take back control, please point that out to me and help me have the courage and strength to resist successfully any temptation or desire to take control again of my life.

Show me how to live on top of my circumstances and not under them. Help me keep my eyes on You, Lord Jesus, instead of on my problems. Let me see You, Father, as the One who can and will meet every need of my life. Let me be sufficient in You and not in my own abilities and strengths. Help me to have the right balance between living in Your control and exercising diligence as I respond to each facet of my life. Whenever pressures come that have been unbearable or debilitating before, show me Your perspective—anything I've been doing wrong or thinking improperly. Then show me how to correct my faulty actions and thoughts so that I can continue to walk in Your Spirit's control. Thank You that You want to do these things in my life even more than I do. Remind me of that when my faith gets weak.

When we make this decision to walk moment by moment in the Spirit's control, it would be wonderful if we never tried to take control of our lives again. But in reality, we do still sin. So what needs to be done at such times is something that Campus Crusade for Christ calls "Spiritual Breathing." This means exhaling the impure—confession of sin, and inhaling the pure—asking the Holy Spirit to once again take control of our lives. We then continue to walk in the Spirit's control.

The crux of the matter is this. The person who allows the pressures of the Rat Race to get to him, to squeeze him into actions and thoughts that are not Spirit led, responds negatively to the Rat Race and is not able to draw on the power and control of the Holy Spirit to stay on top of his circumstances. His circumstances become the main focus of his life, and they knock him about, drag him down, and overwhelm him constantly. *As he looks at his circumstances, his need to cope can make him impatient; he may be short-tempered and in a hurry.* This is not the abundant Christian life that Jesus promises in John 10:10 (KJV) when He says, "I am come that they might have life and that they might have it more abundantly."

You *can* live successfully in any and all circumstances, including the severe pressures that come with the Rat Race. The choice is yours. Depend upon your own strength and abilities or depend on the Holy Spirit flowing through you, who keeps you anchored to the Lord and the solid Rock of Jesus, and keeps you "looking unto Jesus, the author and finisher of our faith" (Heb. 12:2).

Part of learning to live successfully and breaking the cycle of busyness will be to put aside your tendencies for perfectionism. Our need to be perfect in everything before we can be happy is just another form of the Enemy's trap. It adds unnecessary pressures to our lives and makes us rely upon our own strengths and abilities to try to live our lives successfully. Chapter 9 will show you how to recognize and avoid the traps of perfectionism.

Chapter Nine

Put Aside Perfectionism

I was scheduled to speak at a series of denominational meetings in the midwest a few years back and had difficulty finding the conference center. Like any strong-willed American male, I didn't read the map because I thought I knew where I was going. The car I had borrowed was nearly out of gas, and seeing a gas station up ahead, I decided this might be the appropriate time to fill up. But to my dismay, I found myself stranded right in front of the station. A few truckers jumped from their "big rigs" and helped me push the car into the station. The attendant explained that this station was not for cars, but could only be used for large trucks. In fact, he didn't even have a nozzle small enough to fit my vehicle. Even though the fuel to power my car was inches away, I had no way of tapping it. I was helpless.

Many people sense this same frustration in their walk with God. God's strength, His mercy, His grace, and all the resources of the universe may be right at our disposal, but we just can't seem to tap into His resources. God desires to fill vessels, even as small as we are in His sight, but we must be prepared to strengthen our walk with God.

If you are a perfectionist, and you thought we were finished with those items in which you need to grow, I hate to disappoint you. But remember, the fourth warning sign of someone trapped in the Rat Race is perfectionism.

In the first part of this book, I discussed the typical lifecycle of someone who is caught in the Rat Race. A person tends to move from a sense
of inadequacy to a desire for perfectionism rather quickly in search of fulfillment. Inevitably, compulsive behavior follows, leaving the person feeling trapped in the fast track. On this road, each of us will find long-term,
deep relationships to be difficult due to the high expectations placed upon
others. I've encountered perfectionist personalities for years and have
come to realize that not all perfectionists act and think alike.

FOUR KINDS OF PERFECTIONISTS

Some, for instance, are moral perfectionists. Their emphasis is defined
within moral and ethical codes. They tend to pursue their chosen path with
intensity, doing their very best to be true to their belief system in any given
situation. Sadly, what happens is that moral perfectionists turn their reasonable value systems into oppressive sets of rigid rules and regulations that few,
including themselves, can ever completely adhere to. This creates tensions as
the perfectionist becomes critical of others who do not hold the same standards. In the Christian context, The moral perfectionists often are the ones
who are critical of the pastor for not meeting their expectations. They often
will spend long hours in the Word, looking down on those who do not. Too
often they are the ones in the middle of church splits. Unfortunately, they
beat people with the Bible instead of lovingly presenting it.

There are also the appearance oriented perfectionists, who define
themselves by the image they present to the world. Their self-worth is dic-
tated by how they look: their weight, height, the size of their biceps, the
clothes they wear, and where they live. Compliments and other signs of
approval are welcomed, while rejection and criticism are avoided at all
costs. They are their own worst enemy, unless they are satisfied with what
they see, which is rare. When they reach their later years, and their appearance no longer is perfect, these perfectionists can easily become depressed
and permanently dissatisfied with themselves and others unless they have
let the Lord change their values.

Many perfectionists in the Rat Race fall into a third category that I'll
call the achievement oriented perfectionists. Their lives are a constant
search for more accomplishments, greater performance, and higher
achievement. How do they know if all is well? They're winning! They're
outperforming their competitors, getting higher grades, and making more

money. If something cannot be done perfectly, they won't try, but will sense absolute fulfillment when something is completed without a flaw. The driven quality of this perfectionist can sometimes cause others to feel inferior. The amount of time it takes to achieve their goals can rob time from those who are near and dear to them. Unfortunately, these people also have another hurdle that may destroy them—reaching their goals! Why? Because they have been so oriented to striving to catch the gold ring, that when they have it, all the fun, excitement, and challenge of reaching for the top is gone. There is nowhere to go and they are devastated and depressed. Or, having reached the top, they fear that someone is going to try to become "king of the mountain" in their place.

The final type is the relational perfectionist. Their lives are molded and measured by the company they keep. Life is wonderful when the "other people" in their lives do things their way and meet their lofty standards at all times. If these people cannot, the relational perfectionist will nag, correct, and even manipulate to make sure others at least try to meet their expectations. When a competitor appears to be getting ahead in life's race, they will find a way of declaring their opponent a "loser" by locating fatal flaws and glaring inadequacies. The greatest weakness of the relational perfectionist is an inability to make allowances for others. You see, their lives are so neat and orderly, that they cannot have "messy," unpredictable people disrupting the flow. Thus lasting relationships are limited or eliminated. Typically they are the ones who are looking for Prince Charming or Cinderella, and those are few and far between. Their philosophy is, "There's just thee and me and sometimes I worry about thee."

Are you a relational perfectionist? Has this trait trapped you on the fast track to the point of being more lonely now than you've ever been? Here's a simple quiz to help you see if you need to learn how to make allowances for the significant others in your life:

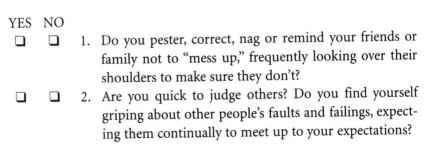

YES NO

❑ ❑ 1. Do you pester, correct, nag or remind your friends or family not to "mess up," frequently looking over their shoulders to make sure they don't?

❑ ❑ 2. Are you quick to judge others? Do you find yourself griping about other people's faults and failings, expecting them continually to meet up to your expectations?

❑   ❑   3. When in the company of other people who appear to superior to you, do you feel uncomfortable or even a little angry?

❑   ❑   4. Do you sometimes see the people in your life as rivals and so you try to "one-up" them often? ("Nice car, but I'm glad I own a BMW.")

❑   ❑   5. Do you associate with less capable or accomplished people to make sure you are on top?

❑   ❑   6. Do you get so impatient with the habits of others that you feel compelled to harp on them just to remind them of your disapproval?

❑   ❑   7. Are you convinced that people should change as soon as you point out what they do wrong, growing increasingly annoyed when they do not?

❑   ❑   8. Have you been irritated or just surprised recently, by someone who has pointed out some constructive criticism or helpful advice?

❑   ❑   9. Has someone said to you lately,
   • "Get off my case!"
   • "Can't I do anything right?"
   • "Who asked you?"
   • "Can't you say anything nice?"
   • "OK, what's wrong now?"

❑   ❑   10. Do you ever complain about not having any real friends?

If you answered seven or more of these questions in the affirmative, you probably have some lessons to learn about making allowances for others. Just think for a moment about our society's commitment to continuing education. As you grew up, you probably were involved in several of the following: music lessons, swimming lessons, golf lessons, tennis lessons, singing lessons, cooking lessons, crafts, or hobbies

Our culture is full of opportunities to learn. But when was the last time you had a class on interpersonal development? Face it, if you are caught in the Rat Race, you will all need to learn or should I say relearn, how to interact with others in your life. What we need to learn are the do's and don'ts of people skills.

One of the richest places to find the keys to developing such skills is the Bible. We will look at this more in depth at the end of this chapter.

THE DILEMMA

Perfectionists find themselves in a real predicament: either learn to make allowances or continue to keep people at arm's length. The real struggle is internal. While the relational perfectionists crave—as all human beings do—unconditionally loving, supportive, and lasting relationships, they often assume they will never have them. Interestingly enough they themselves do not provide that kind of relationship.

Many people stuck in the Rat Race of the nineties were raised in an atmosphere of nonacceptance, where failure and mistakes were taboo and not tolerated. Some were reared by perfectionist parents who generated unrest in the home by "carrot dangling" and expecting more than their children could ever possibly deliver.

Nearly fifty percent of the twenty- and thirty-something generations lost stability of their home life by losing a parent through divorce or abandonment. And although these circumstances were seemingly beyond their control, they still sensed that in some way, they were to blame. So through all the interpersonal turmoil, they began to doubt if closeness and friendships would ever become a reality. Most of those caught in this tragic situation react to relationships in one of the following ways.

Some *project*. "I'm not the problem, you are," becomes their psychological defense. Now, don't get me wrong, these people do not do this intentionally. They simply move from fault finding, to flaw detection, to self-preservation. Here they find the needed reassurance that maybe, just maybe, they're not so bad after all: *If I spend enough time examining everyone else, I will be too busy to inspect myself, and I'll probably never discover my own frailties. And even if I do, I will have discovered so many more in others, that it won't matter about the few I may have.*

Others *reject*. These people have thoughts along these lines: *I know, sometime down the road, I will be hurt in some way by this intimacy and friendship. So before I fall apart at the seams, I'll reject them before they reject me.* There is a keen flaw in this kind of thinking. You still lose a relationship, so nobody wins. Just because you took the offense doesn't diminish the pain, disappointment, and sense of failure. This becomes a self-perpetuating prophecy. "They will. . . . Therefore, I will act first." And when the person sees the expected negative result, they are inclined to say "See, I told you so!"

The rest of them *reflect*. They reflect to others their need to be number one. They encircle themselves with those to whom they may feel superior and they do whatever it takes to stay on top. Their attitudes and actions drive people away. They say to themselves, *No problem—I'll seek out replacements, people who understand and admire my abilities,* starting the whole self-defeating process all over again.

So let's review the many faces of the perfectionist: moral, appearance-oriented, achievement-oriented, and relational. We have seen that the answer to the relational perfectionist qualities is found in making allowances for others.

Beating Perfectionism

But what if every area of your life is caught in the "all-or-nothingism" of the perfectionist's thinking? What if you have reduced your life to a system of black-and-white polar opposites, so that either all is well in your world or nothing is? What if you must achieve complete success—a piece of work flawlessly executed, a relationship with no conflicts in it, your personal best in every race, an "A" on every test? If you are caught in this endless trap of tunnel vision, blaming and shoulds, musts and have-tos, there is only one way you will ever get out of it. You need to stop and spend time alone with God in prayer and meditate on what He shows you.

There will probably be several areas, in which you will want to seek His input. We will look at four common ones.

Establish Your Priorities

Sometimes we get so caught up in our perfectionist ways that we neglect critical areas of our lives. When we get out of balance in any of the following five priorities, we are in trouble. By bringing them back into God's perspective and balance, we can often intercept the perfectionist tendencies that may be there because we are weak in one or more of these five areas:

Spiritual Health. We need to have quality time with the Lord. This means that if we are not regularly praying and reading the Word we well may find ourselves trying to compensate by *doing* things for God, pushing ourselves to accomplish things that please Him. Too often we buy into the Enemy lie that the things we do for God are the most important things. Spending time with Him can sometimes seem less important than our witnessing, teaching Sunday School class, or serving on church commit-tees. The visible becomes more valuable in our minds than the less visible. But God's priorities are exactly the opposite. He wants us to spend time with Him so we can in turn be and do what He wants. We have to grow in Him to stay spiritually healthy.

Emotional Health. Oftentimes, we try to get our self-worth from the wrong source—accomplishments. When we feel uncertain about our acceptance before God or with others, we can get caught in the trap of per-formance, which leads to perfectionism. What we need to do is to know who we are in Christ. There are many wonderful statements in Scripture telling us just that. For example, "For he chose us in him before the creation of the world to be holy and blameless in his sight" (Eph. 1:4). We are dear-ly loved (John 3:16) and highly valued according to the parables Jesus tells about the hidden treasure and the pearl of great price (Matt. 13:44–46).

Another misconception in the area of emotional health is that we have to be perfect in order for God to be pleased with us. But if we will look at Ephesians 1:6 (KJV) we read that we are "accepted in the beloved." This acceptance is not because of what we do but rather because of who Jesus is and the fact that we are in Him if we have invited Him into our lives as Lord and Savior. Therefore even perfectionists can and should be willing to risk falling short of perfection when they attempt to do what the Lord has asked them to do. Emotionally, it is very helpful to keep our eyes on Jesus, do what He asks, and not worry about the results. Leave the results in His hands. When we do this, we free ourselves from many traps of the Enemy such as worrying about what others think, or beating up on our-selves when we don't measure up to perfection.

It is also encouraging for perfectionists to remember that God is in the process of perfecting us. He uses even our mistakes to help us grow. If you're trying to beat perfectionism, it's helpful to realize that God doesn't expect you to be perfect. Why place on yourself expectations beyond what God asks?

Social Health. People need to be made a higher priority than things. Perfectionists too often strain relationships by demanding the same high standards of others as they do themselves. Just as emotionally we have to see and accept ourselves as God sees and accepts us, so also we have to let others be imperfect and make mistakes. In other words, we have to give others the same permission to be less than perfect that God gives us. If we don't, we will end up alienating people. Good friends need to have permission to be themselves and not feel on guard all the time, lest they offend a perfectionist friend. Regard your friendships as treasures.

Intellectual Health. God has given each of us one or more abilities. But as with any talent, it takes time to develop the skills necessary to do well in an area in which we are gifted. Fear of failure can cause perfectionists to lose out on much that God wants them to do because they are not willing to take risks and be seen as less than perfect.

Seek the Lord's Help in Dealing with Perfectionism

Begin by identifying those areas in which you are a perfectionist. Then ask the Lord to show you *why* you are a perfectionist. Are you insecure, fearful, trying to please, wanting a sense of accomplishment and meaning? After you identify the sources of your perfectionism, ask God to help you overcome them. Share your discoveries with your spouse or a trusted friend and enlist their help as you try to overcome.

Learn to Relax

Relax Your Mind. One of the things that is crucial in avoiding the pressures of the Rat Race is to free your mind from the anxieties of the day. I have a "dump tree" which serves this purpose. It is a large tree overhanging a stop sign on the way home. Were I to carry home all the problems that I confront during the day, I would be no fun to be with. Each day, as I drive past that tree on my way home, I mentally "dump" all the concerns of the day at the base of the tree. The next day as I return to church, I "pick them up" as I pass by the tree.

Relax Your Body. Part of being able to cope well with life is to get enough rest. When we are tired, we become inefficient. Too often we let ourselves be so driven in our perfectionist desires that we end up burning the candle at both ends, and our spark soon flickers. We need to learn to pace ourselves, even to schedule rest and recreation in order to avoid the tyranny of perfectionism.

Admit that You Are Not God

Our Enemy loves to get us to play God. He did this with Adam and Eve, and he has successfully used this trap ever since. The perfectionist is a perfect candidate for this trap. Perfectionists are very good at controlling their environment. Sadly, since they can possibly control everything, life can seem unmanageable. Do you ever stay awake late when you know you need sleep? Do you ever feel the need to exercise but you don't? Have you ever known something is wrong but you do it anyway? If you say "yes" to these kinds of questions, welcome to the Rat Race.

There are four consequences of being your own god.

1. Fear. Genesis 3:10 tells us that Adam and Eve hid because they were afraid that God would find out they had not been perfect. We allow the fear of not being in control to cause us to take things in our own hands and "play God."

2. Frustration. Some people feel they have to have everything perfect in their life and in the lives of those around them. They become judgmental of those who do not live up to their standards. Frustration becomes a way of life as they see person after person disappoint or fail them. As "general manager of their universe" they want to see everything go as planned, but life just doesn't work that way.

3. Fatigue. It is tiring to be always in control. There is both an emotional drain and a physical drain that envelops those who are constantly trying to make things go their way. Frustration brings weariness. Jonah in the Old Testament became weary trying to play God. He knew what God wanted, but Jonah wanted something else. Jonah did everything in his power to see that things went his way. When they did not, he sat down on the ground, moping and drained of energy, and even asked to die.

4. Failure. When perfectionists try to play God, they doom themselves to the very thing they fear most—failure. No human can play God. Adam and Eve, Abraham, and Jonah all tried and failed. Satan tried to exalt himself above God and failed. Even well meaning Peter failed each time he tried to impose his will on Jesus.

When we decide to take control of our lives—to play God—we often find that God has to let us come to the end of our rope, to have to cry out to Him, before we will turn loose and let Him once again be in control. There is only one God and we cannot usurp His place!

We need to learn how to keep from putting ourselves in the place of God, how to let Him lead us, and how to draw closer to Him so we can avoid all Enemy traps to lure us away from His will for our lives. This we can do as we return to our first love.

Chapter Ten

Return to Your First Love

Part of the reason we drift away from the Lord is because we let our times of prayer and Bible study fall behind. We let other things press in on us and steal our close relationship with the Lord. We are often more focused on ourselves, our problems, and our needs than we are on the Lord. We can get on a lukewarm path without even realizing it. So how do we get back on the right path?

PRAYER: THE SOLUTION TO THE LUKEWARM HEART

One day the disciples made a significant request of Jesus: "Teach us to pray" (Luke 11:1). Now, how strange. We all know how to pray, don't we? But how many of us know how to do miracles? Why didn't Jesus' disciples ask to be taught how to perform miracles, how to heal, or how to cast out demons? If I were there, I might have asked how to be more like Jesus or how to preach with greater power. If prayer is as simple as most seem to think it is, why make such a request? Wouldn't that be tantamount to asking, to be taught to eat or sleep?

The answer lies in the life of Jesus. He valued prayer. He modeled it. He lived a life above reproach and with great power. In fact, his disciples had come to realize a crucial truth—prayer was foundational to all Jesus was, and all Jesus did. Jesus was a man of prayer. It saturated everything He did. Jesus prayed as a way of life, not just occasionally. He prayed early in the morning, late at night, all night, during the day, and even while he ministered to people. He "said grace" for His food and the food multiplied.

The power and impact of Jesus' prayer life was not lost on the disciples then or on many believers since. They have all realized that if they really know how to pray, then the results in their own lives and ministries will have much of the miraculous quality that Jesus' life displayed.

A modern-day example is the prayer-saturated life of George Mueller who constantly saw marvelous and often miraculous answers to prayer. Mueller ran many orphanages in the 1900s. When he needed land to build an orphanage but had no money, he wasn't phased. He simply prayed until God miraculously provided it. Mueller was always praying for food for his orphanages. They never missed a meal. Once when they had nothing to eat, he returned thanks for the food, believing God would answer his prayer to supply all their needs. Just then a truck loaded with perishable food broke down in front of his door. On another occasion, as Mueller was on the way to an important speaking engagement, dense fog threatened to block the arrival of the ship on which he was traveling. Suddenly the fog dissipated, just as Mueller had told the unbelieving captain of the ship it would. The ship resumed speed and got him to his appointment on time.

NINE POWERFUL PRAYER SECRETS OF JESUS

So what did George Mueller and Jesus' disciples learn about prayer that unlocked God's power? Jesus' prayer life shows us nine truths that will enable us to allow prayer to saturate our lives and help us overcome the fifth warning sign of the Rat Race—losing our first love.

Prayer Was a Way of Life

For Jesus, prayer was an integral part of daily life, not something He did occasionally. The apostle Paul tells us to pray about everything (Phil. 4:6). "And pray in the Spirit on all occasions with all kinds of prayers and requests" (Eph. 6:18). "Devote yourselves to prayer . . ." (Col. 4:2).

How did Jesus make prayer a way of life?

First, Jesus prayed before an event or incident.

- Before and during His baptism (Luke 3:21–22).
- the word implied a continuous action.
- the baptism immediately preceded the forty days of temptation and fasting in the wilderness.
- Before choosing disciples (Luke 6:12–13).
- Before asking the disciples, "Whom do you say I am" (Luke 9:18–20). This was after many people misunderstood who He was.
- Before His transfiguration (Luke 9:28–29).
- Before Peter sinned so he would not lose his faith (Luke (22:31).

Second, He prayed during ministry.

- Raising of Lazarus (John 11:42).
- During feeding of five thousand and four thousand (Mark 6:41; 8:7).
- When speaking of His upcoming crucifixion (John 12:28).
- After feeding the five thousand (Matt. 14:23).

Finally, He prayed right after times of ministry when most would have been tired and wanting to sleep.

In Prayer Jesus Learned His Father's Will, Then Followed It

Prayer was crucial to Jesus' success. His life on earth gave us the perfect example of what God intended humans to be. Jesus modeled the role of prayer in our lives. Thus He was careful always to approach everything in prayer, praying according to the Father's will, and following whatever the Father showed Him to do. In fact, He clearly lets us know this when he in essence says: "I do only what I see the Father doing" (John 5:19). Jesus, knowing He had prayed within the Father's will, often thanked God ahead of time for the answer.

- Lazarus, in accordance with 1 John 5:14–15.
- Promised the Comforter before praying it (John 14:16).

Jesus Prayed Intensely

Because Jesus was fully human (as well as fully divine), His emotions were human. The intensity of His prayer life can be seen in the amount of time He gave to it. In Luke 6:12 we see Him praying all night. In Mark 1:35, He goes out to pray while it is still dark.

The Scripture records in Luke 10:21 that He was full of joy as He prayed to thank the Father for the tremendous success of the seventy disciples He had sent out.

John captures well the deep emotions that Jesus was feeling as He looked to the cross and all the pain and separation it would bring. He prayed, "Now my heart is troubled, and what shall I say? 'Father, save me from this hour'? No it was for this very reason I came to this hour. Father, glorify your name!" (John 12:27–28).

That emotion is intensified in the Garden of Gethsemane to the point that Jesus' prayer became "agony," which caused Him to sweat drops of blood (Luke 22:44).

Jesus Often Prayed in Solitude

Jesus knew the need to be alone and to spend solitary time with the Father in order to cope with the tremendous load of His ministry. Here was a man who was perfect, sinless. Yet He was living in a fallen, sinful world. He had to interact with evil, vile men who wanted nothing more than to see Him dead. He lived and ate daily with the one who would betray Him to His enemies. Jesus was constantly rejected by the ones He loved so much and for whom He would soon die. People sought Him out all the time, pressed in on Him, accused Him, misunderstood Him, and tested Him. Even then some complained He was not spending enough time with them. How easily He could have let the world's Rat Race destroy His ministry. But He did not.

Being the Creator and knowing what is best for us, Jesus knew the value of drawing aside. Sometimes these solitary times were long, sometimes only a few hours. Here are some of the occasions He drew apart:

- After feeding the five thousand (Matt. 14:22–23). The grammar here clearly shows that Jesus deliberately sought solitude. He dismissed the crowd and sent the disciples ahead of Him in the boat.
- After the Jews were offended by Him and before choosing the twelve disciples (Luke 6:12).
- Before asking the disciples who they thought He was (Luke 9:18).
- In the garden of Gethsemane (Matt. 26:36–44). This time of prayer in Gethsemane was crucial to Jesus being able successfully to handle the

pressures of the hours leading to the time of His death. This prayer was a time of strengthening, recommitment, and submission of His will to that of the Father.

Jesus Prayed for Himself and Others

We don't know the content of many of His prayers, but undoubtedly they contained much that was personal. We do know that in the model prayer He gave the disciples, there is ample prayer for personal needs— food, forgiveness, avoidance of temptation, deliverance from evil.

There are other times that Jesus prayed for Himself:

- When contemplating the cross (John 12:28).
- On the cross, two times. "My God, my God, why have you forsaken me?" (Matt. 27:46) and "Father, into your hands I commit my spirit." (Luke 23:46).

He prayed for others and let them know He was praying for them:

- The disciples to receive the Holy Spirit (John 14:16–17).
- Peter (Luke 22:32).
- Us (John 17).
- On the cross when He asks for forgiveness for what was being done to Him (Luke 23:34).
- Raising of Lazarus (John 11:41–42).

As an extension of His earthly ministry, He now intercedes for us at the right hand of God the Father (Heb. 7:25; 1 John 2:1).

Prayer Empowered Jesus in Times of Pressure and Crisis

Pressure can kill us no matter what the source. Jesus knew the importance of taking breaks to be away and to recharge His spiritual batteries from the Father. It is always such a delight to be with one you love. For Jesus, I am sure, these times with His Father were like a life line to rescue Him from the unnecessary pressures of the world.

But were these times infrequent? The Greek word in Luke 5:15–6 that tells us that Jesus "withdrew" when the crowds pressed in on Him implies habitual action. Thus William Hendriksen concludes, "So again and again, Jesus would withdraw himself and steal away to lonely places. This withdrawal also had a positive purpose, namely, to pour out his heart in prayer in order that the reservoirs of his body and soul might be replenished from his Father's inexhaustible resources." [1]

We see Jesus take this same step when tension and opposition ran high after He healed a man with a withered hand on the Sabbath (Luke 6:11–12). He sought solitude and strengthening of prayer by going out to the mountainside to spend the night through prayer. (How many of us spend all night in prayer when we face negative circumstances or a crisis?)

Crisis with its resultant temptations can often be difficult to handle. We often get overwhelmed with the problems. We focus so much on the problem, that we block out the Lord. Our thinking gets fuzzy and we feel overwhelmed, and even confused. Yet when the Jews prematurely wanted to take Jesus and make Him king, He faced the crisis by removing Himself from the temptation to bypass the cross. Instead of yielding, He prayed (Matt. 14:22–23).

How many times do we pray during a crisis? Oh, yes, we pray, but the question is when? Too often I catch myself in either the middle of a storm or at my wit's end, only then remembering to bring God into the problem. We, too, need to pray as soon as we realize we are in a crisis, long before it is able to overwhelm us or to steal our peace of mind.

Jesus Knew that Prayer was a Key to Ministry

I am convinced that without the great amount of prayer Jesus offered, He would never have been able to do many of the things that He accomplished. He says as much in Matthew 17:21 when His disciples are embarrassed and confused about not being able to cast out the demons in a young boy. Jesus tells them these things come out only by prayer and fasting. The fact that Jesus was able to do it and the disciples were not says something about the prayer life of both Jesus and the disciples.

Jesus makes some heavy-duty promises about other important things that would happen when believers pray. Among them are: the following "And all things, whatever you ask in prayer, believing, you will receive." (Matt. 21:22, NKJV); "Ask and it shall be given unto you . . ." (Matt. 7:7, KJV). Such promises may have seemed a little out of their reach at the time, but history would show that this is exactly what happened.

Jesus Prayed Specifically and to the Father

When Jesus prayed, it was not to "the Great power in the sky" or "mother earth." He prayed to the Father. Now, was He ever ambiguous in what He asked? When Jesus prayed for Peter to make it through his trial, Jesus did not say, "Lord, help Peter be strong." Instead, in Luke 22:32 Jesus tells Peter that He had prayed that Peter's faith would not fail, and that when he turned back, he would strengthen his brothers. In a similar manner, Jesus specifically requested that the Holy Spirit be given to indwell all believers as a Comforter. Is it any wonder that such specific prayers had specific answers?

Jesus' Purpose in Prayer Was to Glorify the Lord

God is worthy of our praise and thanksgiving. Jesus, who was very God Himself, still acknowledged that as man, He needed to glorify the Father and thank Him for what He does.

When predicting His own death in John 12:28, Jesus says, "Father, glorify your name!" Was this a one-way prayer conversation? No, the Father responded audibly to Him saying, "I have glorified it, and will glorify it again."

Even in simple things such as returning thanks for food, we always see Jesus, acknowledging God as the source of the blessing.

His praise and thanksgiving to God are evident when He hears the news of the great success of the seventy who went out in ministry (Luke 10:21).

Did Jesus' discipline of prayer help Him live beyond the Rat Race? Unquestionably it did. There are four basic reasons:

1. He had perfect communication with His Father who knew and guided Jesus in exactly how He should live His life to avoid any traps.
2. Jesus knew who He was. This gave Him the confidence not to be intimidated or drawn away from His purposes.
3. Jesus' life was righteous because He chose not to yield to temptation. Prayer and right use of Scriptures became integral parts of resisting such temptation.
4. When pressures came that could take Him off track or cause Him to be caught up in the Rat Race, Jesus instead withdrew, often to the mountains: here, He spent time with His Father, learning His perspective so He could avoid any pitfalls the Enemy had laid for Him.

With these four reasons in mind, let's take a closer look at fourteen reasons why Jesus was not caught up in the Rat Race.

Jesus — Our Model

As we grow up we follow many models—parents, teachers, even our older siblings and peers. Our models can be good or not so good. But in Jesus we have a perfect model. By imitating His qualities, we, too, can avoid the traps of the Race.

1. Jesus knew who He was and what His mission was and therefore was able successfully to handle the Enemy.
   - Knew He must about His father's business (Luke 2:49).
   - Did not choose to defend His Deity while being tempted (Luke 4:3–4).
   - Claimed who He was by His "I Am" statements (John 6, 8–11, 14, 15).
   - Knew His role as the Son of Man (Matt. 8:20; 11:19; 12:8, 40).
   - Knew He was not of this world (John 8:23).
   - Was willing to give up all the privileges of Deity and be humble as a servant (Phil. 2:5–8).
   - Was willing to suffer the death on the cross (Luke 23:33).
2. He was not intimidated by the Enemy or the world.
   - He did what He knew was right, even though others did not agree. A person caught in the Rat Race often performs for others because he desires their approval and gains his own self worth through what he does.
3. He was a man of prayer—all of the time.
4. He did only what He saw the Father doing.
   - He knew exactly what He was to do and did it no matter what happened. He focused on God, not man.
5. He was a servant (Matt. 20; 27).
6. He was filled with the Spirit and showed forth the fruit of the Spirit.
7. He cared about others.
   - You read little about His taking care of His own interests. He was always focused on others. Yet undoubtedly He never made a move without knowing that God was directing it and knowing the move fit into God's plans for that moment. "I must be about My Father's business." (Luke 2:49). "He must needs go through Samaria." (John 4:4, KJV)
8. He took time out to rest after long, intense hours of ministry (Luke 5:15–16).
9. He delegated authority when it was needed. As Jesus' ministry

developed, He did not try to do everything Himself. He equipped others so they could go out and be part of the ministry.
- Trained the twelve disciples.
- Sent the seventy out to minister.
- Had a disciple get the donkey for Him for the Triumphal Entry.
- Preparation for the Last Supper.

10. Jesus was not afraid to chose someone to follow Him who would never succeed or others who would make bad mistakes at times.

When you look closely at the relationship between Judas and Jesus, you are struck by the loving way in which Jesus treats this one who "is a devil" (John 6:70). Jesus knew men's hearts (Luke 9:47), so in choosing Judas, He must have known what kind of man Judas was, especially since he was chosen only after Jesus spent the night in prayer. Yet Jesus gave him the supreme opportunity to change, even giving him a position of honor and responsibility among the disciples by making him treasurer. When Judas came to betray Him, Jesus knew full well his intent. Still the Scriptures use specific Greek words that describe an embrace and kiss that is only given to close friends. What more could Jesus have done to offer a sinner and rebel the opportunity to change?

But even with all this, Judas never repented; he never submitted his will to the Lord. He was a thief and eventually a betrayer of the One who had given him unconditional love.

I doubt if I could have been so loving had I been in a similar situation, knowing the agony of the cross to which he was betraying me. Jesus did not respond negatively to people or to the circumstances of life—He handled them perfectly because He was focused on God and His will.

Peter also failed Jesus, but the loving Son of God always was patient with him, giving correction, forgiveness, and encouragement where needed.

11. Jesus focused on what He was to do.
- "I must be about My Father's business" (Luke 2:49, KJV).
- "My time has not yet come" (John 7:6, KJV).
- "I must needs go through Samaria" (John 4:4, KJV).

12. He knew how to keep that delicate balance between work, rest, and time with God.
- All three were in proper perspective and balance. None were over emphasized to the hurt or exclusion of others.

13. At times He did not do everything that could be done in the situation.
    • At the pool of Bethesda, many were sick but only one was healed (John 5:1–13).
    • Jesus left a place of ministry where the people wanted more, to go to another place (Matt. 16:4; 21:17).
14. He didn't worry or fret and thereby lose energy and focus.

Jesus was misunderstood, berated for doing good, rejected, betrayed, deserted by friends, and faced a horrible death. But through it all, He kept focused on God's will and God's provision.

So we can see that Jesus employed many ways to avoid the pressures of the Rat Race. These fourteen points make a good foundation by which to evaluate our own lives. Therefore, it would be a healthy exercise to stop right now and do a self-evaluation by asking yourself the following questions:

SELF-EVALUATION

1. Have I sought the Lord and actually heard from Him what it is He wants me to do in my current situation? If applicable: Were the things that put me in the position (job, situation, etc.) led by the Lord or did I choose to get involved in this on my own, and assumed that He would agree? If so, what steps can I take to correct that mistake?

2. How much am I concerned about what others think of me or my actions when I know that what I am doing is what God wants me to do? Am I a man-pleaser more than a pleaser of God?

3. How is my prayer life? Is prayer the first thing I think about during the day as I face problems or difficulties?

4. Do I go to God first in prayer about decisions or only after I see problems coming? How much do I let others influence my decisions and actions?

5. Do I have a servant attitude, or do I need to be served by others? Am I willing to help others even when it is inconvenient or causes me not to get to do something I wanted to do?

6. How much have love, joy, peace, patience, and other fruits of the Spirit been a part of my life recently, especially at home and on the job?

7. Am I really interested in the welfare of others? Do I put others before myself, or am I more self-centered?

8. Am I getting enough rest, or am I more driven than I should be? Do I feel guilty when I'm not doing something "productive"?

9. Am I trying to do too much by myself? Do I let others help me when they can? Do I trust others to do as good of a job as I can? What can I delegate to others?

10. Do I avoid being with people who do not always agree with me or who I know dislike me? Do I give them a chance, or do I simply decide ahead of time what they will do, or say? Do I hold back in decisions that I know to be God's will because I am afraid either of what others may think or of damaging my reputation?

11. Am I easily pulled off by others to do their will and thus fail to do what I know God has for me to do? Do I always consult the Lord first about doing something unplanned?

12. How is my quiet time coming? Do I consider it to be a priority even when pressures come and my time is crowded? How is my relationship with the Lord? Is it growing, treading water, or losing ground? Why? What do I plan on doing to correct any "non-growth" factors or those things that are interfering and holding me back from drawing closer to Him?

13. Do I live on a performance basis? Do I feel guilty when I can't don't do everything there possibly is to do?

14. What am I truly worrying about? How is this affecting my emotions, my health, my sleep, and my relationships?

FOLLOWING JESUS' EXAMPLE

So what does this mean to us today? I can just hear you say, "Sure, Jesus could do this; he was God. But what about me? How can I avoid the Rat Race? It seems so inevitable. How can I return to my first love?" The following nine principles should help you do just that. They are designed to follow the example of Jesus and help you make prayer more alive and relevant to your life.

1. See prayer as a time of developing a close relationship with a wonderful, desirable person who is eager to have such a relationship. In James 4:8, the Lord says to draw near to Him and He will draw near to you. Expect to learn more about God or to start feeling deeper things towards Him. This may be gradual process, so don't be concerned about immediate results. Remember, when you are always trying to evaluate every little element a relationship, the very evaluation can slow the process down. Acting naturally, yet determinedly will be the key.

2. Understand that this prayer time is helping develop spiritual maturity and fine tuning your spiritual life.

3. Know that prayer is your life line to success in your race. Prayer will help set your course straight for the day and help you receive input from your wise Coach.

4. Make prayer your highest priority.

5. Determine that your time in prayer will be enjoyable and that you will come away with something of value. Because the Word is a vital part of the prayer process, when you pray, ask the Lord to show you one meaningful truth for your life from your Bible reading. The Psalms, Proverbs, and Paul's letters are gold mines for promises that will encourage you for the day.

6. Recognize that prayer makes your day go better and helps you impact people positively.

7. See prayer as a wonderful problem solver and a way of positively influencing circumstances and people in a way that you could not do so alone.

8. Use variety to keep your prayer life fresh.

- Pray for family and immediate concerns each day. Try taking other concerns such as work, friends, church, missions, and our country and concentrate on one category per day. For example, on Sunday pray for church concerns. On Monday, pray for our political leaders. On Tuesday, pray for friends' needs. On Wednesday, focus on missions. And so on. Clip articles from the newspaper, magazines, or Christian literature. Each day you may want to pray for one item in the news.

- Whenever possible, start out and close your time with praise and thanksgiving. These help keep your eyes on the Lord to show you that He is quite capable of doing in your life what needs to be done. Focus on a different attribute of God each day. On other days, you may want to focus on a name of God and what that description of Him means to your life that.

- Draw from the Scriptures to enhance your prayer times. Pray Scripture back to the Lord, agreeing with the concepts and, when appropriate, telling Him how this applies to your life and what you are currently facing.

9. When you are in a time of crisis, stop and pray. If you can, get alone and away from distraction. We see Jesus doing this in Luke 5:16 and John 6:15.

In the final analysis, many people who are caught in the Rat Race are living their lives for themselves. At times, they will consult the Lord to see what He wants, but even then it is with the view that they will go His way only if that seems best in their eyes. In stark contrast is Jesus who says, ". . . I seek not to please myself but him who sent me" (John 5:30). By following the above nine principles, you should be able to make your prayer life dynamic and a time of refreshing and refuge from the pressures of the Rat Race. Learn to follow Jesus as your model, using prayer as a key part of avoiding the many traps of life.

Chapter Eleven

Build Relationships That Last

In 1945, shortly after the end of the second World War, a young associate pastor named Cliff and his fiancée, Billie, arranged to get married, despite the fact that they had very little money. They managed to scrape together enough funds for a simple wedding and two train tickets to a city where Cliff had been asked to hold a revival with a friend.

Arriving at the city, the newlyweds got off the train and took a cab to their hotel, only to learn that the hotel had been taken over by the military as a rehabilitation center. They were stranded in an unfamiliar city with only a few dollars in their pockets. There was little they could do, so they hitched a ride on the nearby highway. The man who gave them their ride asked the young couple, "Where would you like to be dropped off?" Cliff's answer was somewhat confusing, "We don't know," and he proceeded to explain their situation. The man was sympathetic and offered a suggestion. A few miles down the road was a grocery store owned by a woman whom he knew. He told them that she had a couple of empty rooms upstairs and might be willing to allow them to stay there inexpensively. Cliff realized that this was not the time to be choosy, so he asked the woman for a room. She gave it to them for five dollars, and they were thrilled.

The following day, Cliff practiced his trombone while his beloved played the piano to the delight of the woman who owned the home. By the music they played, the woman soon realized that this young couple were Christians and invited them to spend the remainder of their honeymoon in her house.

By the end of the first week, they had become great friends. The woman mentioned that a young evangelist was speaking at a youth rally nearby and invited them to attend. Upon arriving, they discovered that the regular song leader was sick, so Cliff was asked to take charge of the music for the service. The evangelist turned out to be the young Billy Graham, and the groom was Cliff Barrows. They met that evening for the first time and a lifetime partnership was formed. And from the beginnings of that evening, Cliff and Billie Barrows became members of the Billy Graham Evangelistic Association and have been used by the Lord in thousands of crusades around the world. All of this began with the foundation of friendship.

OUR NEED FOR COMMUNITY

At the core of every person is a deep need for community. Strained relationships are the signs of a life that is headed for or trapped in the Rat Race. Strained relationships build barriers between friends and family. Strained relationships create exclusiveness and individualism. But you were designed by God to desire to be with other people, to need to belong and be accepted by others. But not all relationships are on the same level. This is what community is all about.

There are different levels of friendship. Examine the following types of friendship and determine how deep are the relationships in your life.

There are *activity-based friendships*. These relationships are founded upon common activities such as shopping, raising kids, hobbies, or even studying. This level of friendship is necessary, but does not necessarily mean that the other person knows the "real you."

A second kind of friendships is what I call *historical friendships*. These are the people with whom we have been connected for many years, maybe even as far back as our youth. The intimacy level never goes very deep because the tie with them is merely a common background, not authenticity and openness.

Professional friendships make up the third category. These include your work associates, other parents at your child's school, and those people in your life with whom contact will only occur when a task must be accomplished. There probably will never be a need to reveal feelings or inner struggles in such settings because the project at hand is more the focus than are the people.

Friendships based upon shared activities, historical ties, and professional interaction are wonderful, but unless superficiality is overcome, these friendships will never be enough to cope with life and its demands. What must also be included in our closest circle of friends are those with whom we can openly and honestly share what is really going on with us on the inside. I'm not talking about the need to have "complaint buddies," but rather the deep need for all of us to have the fourth level—*Community friendships.*

Community friendships require us to make major breakthroughs. We cannot hide our fears, but instead we must push through them to open up and allow ourselves to be vulnerable to others. This is no easy task, but the benefits of community friendships are worth the effort for several reasons.

Community friendships are the safety net for our hearts. You can rest assured that no matter what happens in the family or in our career, friends like these are always going to be there. And the great thing to remember is that the supply is seemingly unlimited. A number of community friendships guarantees a shoulder to cry on and a voice to remind us that we are never alone and that we are accepted just as we are.

Community friendships are a primary way by which to learn how to develop other relationships in our life. With the help of a rich pool of community friendships, we have a basis on which to work out our insecurities and fears, and we can gather the strength, love, and support that is necessary to develop new friends. With this type of fellowship, we can carry out the same healing attributes with parents, mates, children, coworkers and even the strangers with whom we will have contact every day of our lives.

Finally, community friendships allow us to look inside of ourselves. In our open attempt to tell our friends who we really are and what we are really feeling, we are challenged to reflect upon those issues and explain them to ourselves as well. Remember, there is no growth without learning, and there can be no learning without feedback. Genuine friendships provide a valuable source of feedback. Most of the time, we take feedback from friends much better than from family or acquaintances. Friends won't allow us to get away with those things that cause us to withdraw from others and protect ourselves. Real friendships, community friendships, demand the truth about who we are.

Jonathan and David

I love the story of Jonathan and David. Their first face-to-face encounter is recorded in 1 Samuel 17 as Jonathan stood listening to David's discussion of his battle with Goliath. Before long, these two men would become great friends. This friendship did not just happen, however. Their friendship, like any community friendship, grew through five distinct stages.

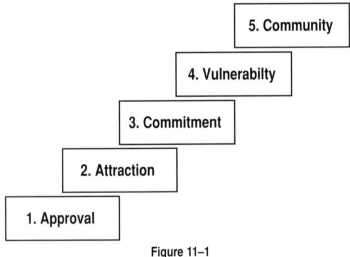

Figure 11–1

Approval

Jonathan possessed the powerful ability to see the potential in others and to judge them for who they were. Don't forget that Jonathan was the king's son. He was a great leader and a proven warrior. A friendship with David would have been very unlikely. David normally was probably much younger than Jonathan; David was a mere shepherd, a "nobody" compared to Jonathan.

Yet Jonathan did not look down upon David and never perceived him as a potential rival. Jonathan's approval of this young shepherd boy was based upon something entirely different. Jonathan was interested in the character of David, not in the external class distinctions of his day.

Many friendships today are based upon power, position, pedigree, and prestige. But Biblical approval is entirely different. Galatians 6:9–10 tells us, "Let us not become weary in doing good, for at the proper time we will reap a harvest if we do not give up. Therefore, as we have opportunity, let us do good to all people, especially to those who belong to the family of believers." We are called to approve and accept our fellow believers long before we meet them, the way God, Himself, accepts us. Romans 15:7 shares, "Accept one another, then, just as Christ accepted you, in order to bring praise to God."

Attraction

David was very honest and open with his feelings. Evidently this trait caused Jonathan to be drawn to David. We are told in 1 Samuel 18:1, "After David had finished talking with Saul, Jonathan became one in spirit with David, and loved him as himself." In fact Scripture tells us that they loved each other. Now, there's a scary term with which to describe friends these days. Some have misunderstood Jonathan and David's relationship to be homosexual. How could God call David a man after His own heart if he were involved in that blatant a sin? Scripture records that the Lord was with David (1 Sam. 18:14). This friendship was not homosexual; this was a biblical model of a real friendship. Friends are naturally attracted to one another. Real friendship, like Jonathan and David's, goes beyond a superficial kind of attraction (based solely on perceived needs and external expectations) and builds upon a commonalty based on each friend's relationship with the Lord. Jonathan and David were "one in spirit" (1 Sam. 18:1).

Commitment

We read in 1 Samuel 18:3 these precious words: "And Jonathan made a covenant with David because he loved him as himself." What kind of covenant? A covenant of friendship.[1] This was a serious commitment.

They were going to do whatever it took to make their friendship a priority in their lives.

We do not see this type of commitment very often in today's society. Our relationships seems to fall somewhere on a commitment continuum symbolized by this chart:

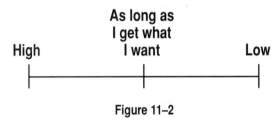

Figure 11–2

No relationship can maintain a constantly high level of energy all of the time. In twenty years of ministry, I have seen numerous married couples who were struggling to rekindle the passion in their marriages. But passion isn't the same thing as commitment. Relationships have become as disposable as diapers and razors. When the passion is low, so is the commitment, and divorce soon becomes an option. The same is true in friendships. Just because there is a disagreement or a falling-out, there does not have to be a lessening of the commitment level. Real commitment is a constant, not in a state of flux. Real community friends are not looking for the back doors to their relationships in the midst of difficult circumstances. Why? Because as Proverbs 17:17 says, " A friend loves at all times, and a brother is born for adversity."

Vulnerability

We read in 1 Samuel 18:4, "Jonathan took off the robe he was wearing and gave it to David, along with his tunic, and even his sword, his bow and his belt." There is great symbolism in this action. In stripping himself of his royal regalia and placing it upon David, Jonathan was recognizing David's divine election to be the future king of Israel. What a risk this was for Jonathan. Yet as a vulnerable person, Jonathan did not think of himself as better than David. He did not worry about his own position, even though he must have known that Samuel had already anointed David as king—the very position that Jonathan should have assumed on his father's death. Jonathan was a humble man, a true friend who knew that there is no community friendship without the risk of being vulnerable.

If I choose to open my heart to a friend and remove my own personal armor of protection around me, I am inviting the other person to see the "real" me, exposed and unarmed. To overcome such reservations, it is helpful to remind ourselves of the great benefits of the community friendships which reduce the risk by inviting others to become our allies.

Community

There comes a point at which friendship is enjoyed without fear of rejection. This point is where community becomes a reality. "Whatever Saul sent him to do, David did it so successfully that Saul gave him a high rank in the army. This pleased all the people, and Saul's officers as well" (1 Samuel 18:5). There was no threat, no envy, and no seeking of revenge toward David.

Envy is a powerful taskmaster and is much different than jealousy. Where jealousy says, "I want what you have," envy says, "Not only do I want what you have, but I also want you to lose what you've already got." Jealousy says, "I want my grass to turn greener than yours," where envy says, "And not only that, but I want your grass to turn brown." There is no room for this in a genuine setting of community, as Jonathan was able to model for us in the Bible. Jonathan merely had the very best in mind for his friend and was willing to support him all along the way.

BUILDING COMMUNITY FRIENDSHIPS

Pat Riley, one of the most successful basketball coaches of our era, says, "I'm persuaded that teamwork is the key to making dreams come true. We all play on a number of teams in our lives—as part of a family, as a citizen, as a member of a congregation or corporation. Every team has a covenant, written or unwritten. It contains the values and goals for every team member."[2] In other words, teamwork is community.

How can you develop community friendships?

1. Challenge yourself and others to grow. Paul wrote the church in Ephesus and told them, "As a prisoner for the Lord, then, I urge you to live a life worthy of the calling you have received" (Eph. 4:1). The challenge? Grow into the men and women God wants us to be. The Lord Jesus gave a similar challenge to Paul. The apostle was traveling on the Damascus road, en route to persecute Christians, when a blinding light stopped him in his tracks. In recounting this experience, Paul shares, "Then I asked, 'Who are you, Lord?' 'I am Jesus, whom you are persecuting,' the Lord replied. 'Now get up and stand on your feet. I have appeared to you to appoint you as a servant and as a witness of what you have seen of me and what I will show you. I will rescue you from your own people and from the Gentiles. I am sending you to them to open their eyes and turn them from darkness to light, and from the power of Satan to God, so that they may receive forgiveness of sins and a place among those who are sanctified by faith in me'" (Acts 26:15–18). God's challenge to Paul was to be a servant and witness to the Gentile world.

2. Share your confidence in others. Life runs more smoothly when others show confidence in us. Remember how our Lord did this with Peter? "When Jesus came to the region of Caesarea Philippi, he asked his disciples, 'Who do people say the Son of Man is?' They replied, 'Some say John the Baptist; others say Elijah; and still others, Jeremiah or one of the prophets.' 'But what about you?' he asked. 'Who do you say I am?' Simon Peter answered, 'You are the Christ, the Son of the living God.' Jesus replied, 'Blessed are you, Simon son of Jonah, for this was not revealed to you by man, but by my Father in heaven. And I tell you that you are Peter, and on this rock I will build my church, and the gates of Hades will not overcome it'" (Matt. 16:13–18). Peter . . . a rock? Not the Peter I read about. Peter only opened his mouth long enough to exchange feet. He was impulsive, not an immovable rock. But our Lord's confidence extended far beyond Peter's struggles and failings. Our Lord knew that it would be Peter who would deny Him three times. Our Lord knew that he would have to say to Peter, "Get thee behind me Satan" (Matt. 16:23, KJV) when Peter rebuked Jesus concerning our Lord's explanation of His upcoming death, burial, and resurrection. And yet this frail, unimpressive man would be entrusted by the Son of God with a major role in the early Christian church.

When you talk with others, see their potential, not just their problem areas. Anticipate something good in their lives and convey your confidence in them. Any good teacher knows that this is the key to changing many a problem child into a positive, happy, integrated part of the classroom.

3. Make encouragement a priority. My wife taught history at the high school level for ten years. Nancy is the eternal optimist. Her early philosophy of education was to find students doing something well and then encourage them to continue. Why? Because all of us need encouragement, the feeling that we are worthwhile in someone else's eyes.

How Paul needed encouragement from Barnabas, "the Son of Encouragement"! Can you imagine the shattered image Paul must have had of himself when he finally realized the truth about who Jesus is? It was bad enough that he had rejected Jesus, let alone that he had actively sought out believers and brought them to Jerusalem to be mocked, often tortured and then killed. Probably Paul was the one at whose feet were cast the cloaks of those who were stoning Stephen (Acts 7:58).

Barnabas took Paul under his wing, introducing him to other believers and sticking up for him when Paul had yet to prove the truth of his changed ways. God alone knows how different church history might have been had Barnabas not been there to encourage Paul to be the leader he was to become.

4. Correct others lovingly. I have always believed that progress will follow feedback. There will be times when you will need to lovingly build up people while correcting them; our Lord did. In Mark 9, Jesus had just come down from the Mount of Transfiguration where Peter, James, and John had seen Jesus in His glorified state. Coming to the base of the mountain, they must have seen the other disciples huddled together and arguing with other people. Evidently the disciples had tried in vain to cast a demon from a boy who was having seizures. Jesus told them to bring the boy to Him.

> So they brought him. When the spirit saw Jesus, it immediately threw the boy into a convulsion. He fell to the ground and rolled around, foaming at the mouth. Jesus asked the boy's father, "How long has he been like this?" "From childhood," he answered. "It has often thrown him into fire or water to kill him. But if you can do anything, take pity on us and help us."
>
> "'If you can't?'" said Jesus. "Everything is possible for him who believes."
>
> Immediately the boy's father exclaimed, "I do believe; help me over come my unbelief!"
>
> When Jesus saw that a crowd was running to the scene, he rebuked the evil spirit. "You deaf and mute spirit," he said, "I command you, come out of him and never enter him again."

The spirit shrieked, convulsed him violently and came out. The boy looked so much like a corpse that many said, 'He's dead.' But Jesus took him by the hand and lifted him to his feet, and he stood up.

After Jesus had gone indoors, his disciples asked him privately, 'Why couldn't we drive it out?' He replied, 'This kind can come out only by prayer" (Mark 9:20–29)

Our Lord confronted their unbelief and dependence on personal achievement and abilities. He turned an embarrassing event into a teachable moment . . . with loving correction.

5. **Accept people the way God has accepted you**. God has made many different personality types. Each type responds to situations differently. When we try to change the way God has made people, and try to make them fit the type we are, we can mess things up. Let God be God and you be the human being who makes "every effort to live in peace with all men" (Heb. 12:14).

Horace Fenton rightly concludes, "Who knows how much soul-damage has been done through the centuries by Christians who have passed hasty judgment on the attitudes, actions and motivations of fellow believers! How many families have been destroyed because one member judged another before all the facts were in? How many long-standing friendships have been weakened or even dissolved when the ugly seeds of suspicion were allowed to take root? How many local churches and even denominations have hurt their witness to the world for the same reason?" [3]

6. **Have more fun**. The term "lighten up" is tailor-made for Rat Racers. Friends spend time together doing things that bring them joy. Adding spontaneity, and trying to bring joy to someone else are just two of the many ways we can add fun to our relationships.

7. **Relax**. The statement, "I feel guilty when I relax" had to be coined by a Rat Race participant. Tim Hansel puts it well: "For a Christian there is no such thing as 'free time.' All of the Christian's time is redeemed and belongs to the one who has set us free. Therefore, it is impossible for a committed believer to say his working time is more valuable than his leisure time." [4] He adds, "We have yet to learn that true leisure is not idleness, and that leisure is each man's touchstone with himself and his inner resources. We haven't yet decided how much value to give to the leisure in our lives. As a result we don't know how to put it in a proper balance with work." [5]

Doctors tell us that relaxation is crucial to our well being. God not only instituted a day of rest but modeled it for us. In fact, God stressed this idea of a day of rest so much that He commanded the penalty for the violation of this rule to be death. Archibald Hart in his *Adrenaline and Stress* writes, "Serious business, isn't it? Why? Does it not seem strange to you that God should take the matter of rest so seriously? Was He simply being arbitrary, like a neurotic parent who wants to rob his child of every bit of pleasure? Certainly not. There is great wisdom in all God's commands. We are just too stubborn most times to understand them! But my work with stress patients and my own experience of learning to relax has shown clearly that God's emphasis on rest was for our benefit." [6]

8. Be patient with others. The word *patience* in the New Testament means to have a long fuse. Patience is the ability to see that people, problems, and situations are not always the way you would like them to be, but everything will be all right as you trust in Christ to work all things together for good.

If you genuinely desire to build community friendships, you will need to lay aside your urges to correct and advise. Think through the real importance of what you want to share. Is it that big of a problem? Is the behavior a threat to anyone? More often than not, you will develop greater patience by watching God work and trusting His outcome.

9. Empathize, don't criticize. Making allowances for others will become easier if you can learn to put yourself in another's place. Most of us misunderstand empathy. Some perceive empathy as our ability to carry everyone else's problems. Others see it as an intense withdrawal from life in search of a more sensitive you. Empathy is merely the ability to put yourself in other people's shoes, to see the world through their eyes, to genuinely feel what they may be feeling.

Now, how do you do this? Jesus is our example. So ask the Lord to help you see others as He does. Try to imagine what they might be feeling. What needs or fears could be motivating their behavior? What is behind the words they share with you? Then, look for a time in your life when the same kinds of emotions and fears were stirred up. When a circumstance comes to mind, or a similar experience is remembered, you will have the foundation to be able to understand their behavior. If the person with whom you are trying to empathize is one who is a constant irritation to you, this kind of activity can greatly reduce the conflict allowing a possibly renewed relationship to gain a foothold. Asking the Lord to give you a concern and compassion for those people is also an essential element of empathy.

10. **Repair hurting relationships.** People caught in the Rat Race can wreak havoc on the people around them. Their nit-picking, pessimistic attitudes cause much unwarranted stress and pain in their relationships. When one of your relationships is strained, take the initiative to repair it immediately. Talk the problem over with your friend. Seek or give forgiveness where it is needed. Even difficult times can bring growth in ourselves and our relationships.

A LITTLE EFFORT MAKES A LOT OF DIFFERENCE

A small boy lived by the ocean. He loved the creatures of the sea, especially the starfish, and spent much of his time exploring the seashore.

One day he learned that there would be a minus tide that would leave the starfish stranded on the sand. The day of the tide, the boy went down to the beach and began picking up stranded starfish and tossing them back into the sea.

An elderly man who lived next door came down to the beach to see what he was doing. "I'm saving the starfish," the boy proudly declared. When the neighbor saw all the stranded starfish, he shook his head and said, "I'm sorry to disappoint you young man, but if you look down the beach one way, there are stranded starfish as far as the eye can see. And if you look down the beach the other way, it's the same. One little boy like you isn't going to make much of a difference."

The boy thought about this for a moment. Then he reached his small hand down to the sand, picked up a starfish, tossed it out into the ocean, and said, "I sure made a difference for that one."

You may feel like this little boy, wondering if your desire to build community friendships will make a difference. The answer is, yes, it will a difference to the friends you will make and to you.

Chapter Twelve

Establishing a Life Map

I believe God calls each one of us to have a "parable perspective," to see life as a learning experience, and to recognize that through the common experiences of life, God will reveal something to us. When my children were very young, I can remember driving along a newly paved road not far from home and spying a squirrel that was walking a tightrope across the highway on a telephone line. My initial thoughts were, *What a dumb animal. Doesn't it realize the peril of walking at such heights?* Then Kerry, my daughter, pointed to several squashed squirrels on the road. And God brought to mind a passage of Scripture, "Enter through the narrow gate. For wide is the gate and broad is the road that leads to destruction, and many enter through it. But small is the gate and narrow the road [or wire] that leads to life, and only a few find it" (Matt. 7:13–14). That day, I gained a "parable perspective."

I love the story shared by Nate Adams:

> "There's nothing quite like running in a race and being in the lead. Way out in front of the pack is an exhilarating place. If you've never experienced it, you should round up some slow people and give it a try.
>
> In the lead is where I found myself one day during an eighth-grade track meet. It was a 220-yard run, which in most places is halfway

around the track. I was just coming into the second turn when I was taken with the not-so-humble thought that everyone else in the race was inhaling my dust. A slight wave of cockiness overcame me, and I decided to do what the track coaches tell you never to do—I looked back.

Yep, there were my suffering competitors, several feet behind me and straining hard. I turned back smugly to the home stretch of the race. That's when a fairly large moth flew between the upper and lower boundaries of my prematurely confident grin. It landed right on the back of my tongue, and suddenly the race was the last thing on my mind.

I began spitting, coughing, and hacking, and various moth parts escaped from my mouth with each effort. I actually remember think-ing, "That was a wing! That was a leg! Oh yuck, that was an antenna!" Once moth parts stopped coming out, the feeling of utter disgust set in. I had tasted–and almost digested–an ugly, fluttering insect. It had spent long enough in my mouth for me to dismember it, and who knows what microscopic parts or fluids might still be in me. What kind of doctor does one see for moth poisoning?

Although this all happened in a matter of seconds, I think you can imagine what happened in the race. That guy who was straining so hard in second place and two or three of his buddies passed me up, and I ended up having their dust as a main course for my moth appe-tizer. I lost the race—the race I was winning until then.[1]

Have you ever been so busy, so excited about where you're going, and so consumed with what is on your plate at that moment in time, that you forgot about the destination? Sometimes we are running our own Royal Race and the littlest things of life, even a moth, can throw us off stride if we are not focusing on the finish line, if we have no sense of direction. Suddenly, the whole focus of our race changes as we get sidetracked into the Rat Race. Therefore, what every child of God needs, in order to best facilitate their race, is a life map.

If there were just one gift I could give to the people I meet and the peo-ple I love, it would be the ability to see what God wants to do in their lives and through their lives. I wish I could help them visualize what God wants to accomplish if they would allow His Spirit to gain control and influence their hearts. It would be part of helping them see the good works God has chosen in advance for us to do (Eph. 2:10).

The apostle Paul was this kind of personality. In Romans 15, we can see the clear life map of this great man of God. This life map was fueled by his driving power and passion as he sought God's direction. He wrote, "It has always been my ambition to preach the gospel where Christ was not known, so that I would not be building on someone else's foundation" (Rom. 15:20). Can't you sense his passion? Paul wanted to plant churches, and impact the world for Christ where no other influence had taken place. And this would be his all-consuming vision, his life map, for his entire life. Near the end of his earthly ministry he shared the source of his life map. "So then, King Agrippa, I was not disobedient to the vision from heaven" (Acts 26:19).

LIFE WITHOUT A MAP

Your life map is more than personal goals. It must be more than a long list of desires accumulated during a brainstorming session. You life map is your *God-given* reason for existing. It is why you are here; it is the very reason for life itself. And without a life map, you will find the Rat Race to be a regular part of your lifestyle. Let's examine four attributes of a life without a map.

1. Frustration. Our decade is a decade of choice. Some choices are good, some not so good. I love, for instance, the freedom to choose the kind of cereal I will eat in the morning from the fifty plus choices available at the market. But other decisions are not nearly as delightful. Life is so complex, mainly due to the information explosion we find ourselves in today. Note these signs of the information explosion shared by Dr. Gary McIntosh in *The McIntosh Church Growth Network* newsletter.

> *Computers*: Between 1946 and 1960 the number of computers grew from 1 to 10,000. From 1960 to 1980 to 10,000,000! By the year 2000 there will be over 80,000,000 in the United States alone. The number of components that can be programmed into a computer chip is doubling every eighteen months.

> *Publications*: Approximately 9,600 different periodicals are published in the United States each year. About 1,000 books are published internationally every day. Printed information doubles every eight years. Keeping up with our reading takes on new meaning.

Libraries: The world's great libraries are doubling in size every 14 years. In the early 1300s, the Sorbonne Library in Paris contained only 1,338 books and yet was thought to be the largest library in Europe. Today, there are several libraries in the world with an inventory of well over 8 million books each.

Periodicals: The Magazine Publishers Association notes that 265 more magazines are being published this year than last year, which works out to about one a day if magazine creators take weekends off. Newsstands offer a choice of 2,500 different magazines.

Knowledge: More new information has been produced in the last 30 years than in the previous 5,000. The English language contains roughly 500,000 usable words. That's about five times more than during the time of Shakespeare. Today information doubles every 5 years! By the year 2000 it will be doubling every 4 years!

Yellow Pages: The Pacific Bell Yellow pages is used about 3.5 million times a day. There are 33 million copies of 108 different directories with 41 billion pages of information.

Dictionaries: The new second edition of the Random House Dictionary of the English Language contains more than 315,000 words, has 2,500 pages, weighs 13.5 pounds, and has 50,000 new entries.

Business: U.S. businesses report that half of their work forces have jobs that are information-related. A new position, the CIO or Chief Information Officer, is responsible for managing information in many businesses.

General: Getting a credit card approval in Paris involves a 46,000 mile journey over phone lines that takes place in 5 seconds. In 1985, 2.8 million tons of computer paper was used in offices in the United States, roughly twice the amount used in 1975. A weekday edition of *The New York Times* contains more information than the average person was likely to come across in a lifetime in 17th century England."[2]

In the midst of this complexity, we can find three kinds of people: Those who make things happen, those who watch things happen and those who have no idea at all what's happening. The last two types are very frustrating lifestyles. But when a person has a life map, frustration is reduced. James wrote concerning the double-minded man, "That manshould not think he will receive anything from the Lord; he is a double-minded man, unstable in all he does" (James 1:7). Divided loyalty and divided focus produce frustration.

2. Apathy. What motivates you? What causes you to get up in the morning saying, "Good morning, Lord," instead of "Good Lord, it's morning!"? When your life map is clearly in focus, you have a reason to get out of bed. Too many people run life on emotional flat tires, facing Monday with dread, and wondering how they will make it through the grind.

A life map generates vision. "Where there is no revelation, the people cast off restraint; but blessed is he who keeps the law" (Prov. 29:18). I meet people all the time who have "cast off restraint," and are constantly asking, "Why? Why work? Why try and hold onto this marriage? Why even try? Why? Why?" A life map answers this question. Paul wrote concerning his antidote for apathy, "I press on toward the goal to win the prize for which God has called me heavenward in Christ Jesus" (Phil. 3:14). Paul was saying that he had something to get up for in the morning. A life map provides the energy and the motivation to keep going.

3. Lack of Focus. Focus was Paul's secret. He shares in Philippians 3:13, "Brothers, I do not consider myself yet to have taken hold of it. But one thing I do: Forgetting what is behind and straining toward what is ahead." He's not trying to focus on twenty things simultaneously, but on what his life map dictates. We only have so much time. People with a life map learn to use it wisely by focusing on finishing. Many flit from one project to the next without finishing anything. We need a good dose of concentration.

If you take light and diffuse it, you can light a room, but the light remains weakened in its potential. Yes, it is accomplishing something, but not on the level it could. But when the same light is focused, it becomes a laser, both powerful and intense. Likewise, a life without focus lacks both intensity and power.

4. Individualism. Without a life map, people feel like they are going it alone. What amazes me is to see how others will want to go along with you when you know where you are heading. Again, let's think back to the life of Paul. His vision was to preach where no one else had shared Christ. Would he have obstacles? Yes! Would he encounter some who would have wrong motives? Of course! In fact he shares in Philippians 1:15–16, "It is true that some preach Christ out of envy and rivalry, but others out of goodwill. The latter do so in love, knowing that I am put here for the defense of the gospel." The people in the church at Philippi shared Paul's vision, and so did many others. They were attracted not only to where he was going, but to his heart's desire in getting there.

The Living Bible translates Proverbs 11:27 as, "If you search for good you will find God's favor; if you search for evil you will find his curse." When your life map is in place you will be in the center of God's will. In the body of Christ, there is no place for individualism. We are a family, a fellowship, and each part of the body must function together. Paul says in 1 Corinthians 12:14–18, "Now the body is not made up of one part but of many. If the foot should say, 'Because I am not a hand, I do not belong to the body,' it would not for that reason cease to be part of the body. And if the ear should say, 'Because I am not an eye, I do not belong to the body,' it would not for that reason cease to be part of the body. If the whole body were an eye, where would the sense of hearing be? If the whole body were an ear, where would the sense of smell be? But in fact God has arranged the parts in the body, every one of them, just as he wanted them to be." It is for this reason that we need to find God's life map for our life; if we are created to be a baby toe, we do not go off on our own trying to be a thumb, an ear, or even, a bigger toe. We will truly only be happy when we discover exactly what God has created us to be—nothing less, nothing more.

DISCOVERING YOUR LIFE MAP

A lot of communities have Little League Football programs in the fall of the year. In one such community, two weeks into the season, an armchair coach with a big gut came into the YMCA and wanted to see the person in charge. He said he had just moved to the area and wanted to coach football. Were there any teams? The YMCA director said, "Yes," but the only kids he had left were the runts and the misfits that nobody else wanted.

The coach said that was fine. So he took the runts and the misfits and he began working with them. It was only a week until the first game and he knew he couldn't teach them much. They already knew how to go up the middle, so all week long he worked on blocking. At the game that week, it didn't take long for the other team to figure out their one play. But even though they stopped the runts from going up the middle, the other team couldn't get past their defense. The final score was 0 to 0.

All the next week, they worked on blocking, and going left. Now they had two plays. That week they won because they scored a touchback. During their third week of practice, they worked on blocking and going right. They had three plays and although they didn't win, that week they scored a touchdown.

During the fourth week, though, the coach had to be gone and asked some of the fathers to take over. The Coach got back in town, drove to the field and the game was already underway. He looked out and it was a disaster, it was chaos. It was only the first quarter and the score was already 21 to 0 in favor of the other team. Everybody was going in every direction possible. Seven kids went out for a pass. Nobody blocked. The kids were confused and crying. So he called them all together and asked what's wrong. They said, "We can't remember 31 or 42 or the sweep."

The coach said, "O.K. Then let's just keep it simple. We'll go back to the basics. Go left, go right, up the middle and block." They kept it simple and they stopped the other team from scoring any more points. They were even able to score twice themselves.

The fathers who had been left in charge started to protest, but then one of the other fathers noticed something. He looked down and the coach with the big gut like Norm on Cheers, the coach who had only taught three plays and blocking, had on a Superbowl Ring. It was then that the fathers realized that he knew 31 and 42 and the sweep and a whole lot of other plays, but he also knew the kids and their limitations. He knew you had to start with and build upon the basics. Without the foundation of the basics, everything else falls apart."[3]

This is where we need to start. What are the basics to finding your life map? I believe there are four steps.

FINDING YOUR LIFE MAP

1. Spend time alone with God. One reason why we find ourselves living life without direction is our busyness. "I'm too busy to stop, too busy to plan . . . too busy to even read my Bible." You're on a plane with no navigator, making record time, but you have no idea where you're going.

Why do we double our speed when we lose our way? This was never God's intention. We are told, "'Be still, and know that I am God; I will be exalted among the nations, I will be exalted in the earth'" (Ps. 46:10).

We have to stop and listen; that may mean turning off the television. You may have to go for a long walk. I do not know what the answer will be for you, but I know it must include time with God or you will attempt to formulate this life map under your own power.

2. Identify and understand your giftedness. In Romans 12:6 we learn that, "we have different gifts, according to the grace given us. If a man's gift is prophesying, let him use it in proportion to his faith." Notice who gives you these gifts—God. We don't get to choose, we are not given a menu at the time of our salvation. And genuine fulfillment comes when we can both identify and understand how God has made us. He would never gift you in one way and then lead your life in a totally different direction where you would ignore your giftedness.

My long-time friend and president of Campus Crusade for Christ, Bill Bright, shares, "The tragedy of many Christian lives is that believers are so involved in trying to discover or receive additional spiritual gifts that they are not developing and using their known gifts and abilities to do God's will.

"For this reason, when I counsel in the area of Christian service, I do not suggest going to great lengths to discover spiritual gifts. Rather, I encourage full surrender to Jesus Christ and the importance of being filled with the Holy Spirit. Only then should one seek God's direction in life. Then, by faith and hard work, a person can set out with determination to accomplish that to which God has called him."[4]

So you ask yourself, "How has God made me unique in the Body of Christ? What am I good at? What do I like to do that is easy and enjoyable? Do I like to entertain (gift of hospitality); to help everyone I can (gift of helps); to listen to others in need and be there for them (gift of mercy); to teach or help people see truths for living (gifts of teaching and exhortation). Asking friends or your pastor or some other believer who knows you well what they think your gift is will reveal and help identify your gifting. They often recognize things in you that you may take for granted, when in fact, it is a specific gift of God that lets you operate easily in that area. There are several good books to help you in this process, especially Larry Gilbert's book on spiritual gifts.[5]

When you get to heaven, God is not going to ask you, "Why weren't you more like Billy Graham?" He's not going to say, "I wished you had been a better parent like James Dobson." And He won't even analyze, "Why weren't you a greater leader like Moses or Joshua?" He will want to know why you weren't more like He created you to be, and for which you had the potential to be. But instead, you fell short because you got sidetracked into the Rat Race through apathy, fear, distractions, or any of a number of other of life's detours.

3. Review your past history and experiences. Scripture records that "In all things God works for the good of those who love him, who have been called according to his purpose" (Rom. 8:28). Two important phrases stand out in this passage. The first is "all things." There is a reason for everything that happens in your life, the pain, the abuse, the neglect, the financial chaos—all things. And God's desire is to integrate "all things" into the second primary clause in Romans 8:28, "his purpose." God will never waste a circumstance—never!

Do you realize that God will use your circumstance and your problem to help others who are struggling with the same pain? Speaking of God, Paul writes 2 Corinthians 1:4, "[He] comforts us in all our troubles, so that we can comfort those in any trouble with the comfort we ourselves have received from God." Even as you read this passage, God probably brought to mind something in your past that He allowed to happen, so that you could use it to help others. Don't be afraid of your past, use it for God's glory.

4. Determine your priorities. There are many things in life that are not necessarily wrong, they are simply not necessary. Paul wrote concerning this, "'Everything is permissible'—but not everything is beneficial. 'Everything is permissible'—but not everything is constructive" (1 Corinthians 10:23). I have often found that good things can be the enemy of the very best things. It's a good thing to get to work early and get a jump-start on your day. But you may miss out on your quiet time alone with God, which would be the *best* thing. It's a good thing to serve on ten committees, but you may hurt the best relationship God brings into your life, the one with your family.

You will not have time for everything. You think you do, but you don't. So there will be a definite need to prioritize if you ever plan to discover your life map. You do this by asking yourself, "What should I be doing that is going to have eternal implications?" Jesus gives us the answer in Matthew 6:20 "But store up for yourselves treasures in heaven, where moth and rust do not destroy."

Apart from Almighty God and His redemptive plan, there are only two things that are going to last forever—God's Word and God's people. I must pour myself into learning and growing in my Bible understanding. I must recognize that how I spend my time now may determine where my family, friends, and associates will be spending their eternity. Regardless of your profession, your educational goals, the place where you choose to live, if you are a child of God, your life map will include the Bible and people.

My personal life map is shaped by three distinct desires. First, I desire to be a man of God and to serve Him with a joy and enthusiasm that is contagious to the people around me. Second, I want to raise a godly family, In which Nancy, my wife, feels love and security, and my three kids sense support and encouragement. Lastly, I choose to invest my life in the ministry. There are many vocations that I have admired and studied, but I'll never forget what my brother-in-law said to me nearly two decades ago, "Glen, if God wants you in the ministry and you don't, you'll be miserable." Jack, you were right. So at the end of my life, when I stand before the Lord of Lords, I too will be able to say, "I was not disobedient to the vision You gave me."

IT'S NEVER TOO LATE TO CHANGE!

O.K. You're convinced. You've decided that you need a life map, but you also may be thinking, *I've already lived a goodly portion of my life without one. Isn't it too late now to change? How do I go about it even if I want to? I feel so trapped where I am. I've already blown it, haven't I?* Not so! With God all things are possible. He's just been waiting for you to recognize the need to factor Him into your life. He's eagerly awaiting your step of turning your life over to Him, and letting His Spirit direct you. Now that He has your undivided attention, let's look at what you need to do to change your life.

Let's use the story of Jacob in Genesis 32 to illustrate each of the four phases we need to go through in order to achieve the desired change in our lives and to secure a life map. Up until this point in life, Jacob had lived in his own strength, doing things "his way." But his way brought him to disaster, as he had to flee for his life from a brother he had tricked, and a father he had lied to. As a result of doing things his way, he never again saw his beloved mother, and lived in fear and uncertainty for many years.

Fear diminished his life and he felt caught in the trap of a lifestyle of his own making. Obviously had he known how miserable doing things "his way" would make him, he would have likely sooner sought God's life map for his life.

The first phase is to recognize the problem. For Jacob, who was a self-sufficient manipulator and cheater, God had to show him his need before he could be all God created him to be. We read in Genesis 32:24–25, "So Jacob was left alone, and a man wrestled with him till daybreak. When the man saw that he could not overpower him, he touched the socket of Jacob's hip so that his hip was wrenched as he wrestled with the man." Verse twenty-eight tells us that it was God who was wrestling with Jacob.

Now I don't know much about wrestling, but I do know this: The object of wrestling is to pin a guy down and make him say "uncle." This may well be how Jacob felt. He was in a long fight that lasted until daybreak. It must have seemed like a no win situation.

We wrestle with problems within the areas of relationships, health, internal feelings, finance, or security, to name a few. Have you considered that your current crisis may well be God's way of getting your attention, of wrestling with you because you have so far not yielded to His desire to follow His ways all of the time? Unfortunately, such wrestling matches are often the only way that God can get through to our hard heads and our closed hearts.

But cheer up. A problem is a sign that God cares and is at work in your life. In fact, this is exactly what James 1 and Romans 5 clearly say is true. He is getting ready to change you. He wants to improve your life. Actually, it's just like the mother eagle. When the baby eagles grow, she messes up the nest so that it becomes so uncomfortable that the eagle wants to learn how to fly. The baby eagle would not change if the nest had not become uncomfortable.

Can you identify with the eaglet? Wouldn't you rather stay in your comfortable circumstances than go through the crisis of change that is often necessary to move us out of our comfort zone and into God's perfect will for us? How many of us say, "One of these days I'll really make that change. One of these days when the circumstances are better." But unless God brings a crisis, chances are that "one of these days" will never come. In fact, we will never change until the problem or pain becomes greater than the fear of change. God may love you just the way you are, but He loves you too much to have you stay that way! And so, if it takes a problem to change you, God will use it for your best.

The fact is that God does use problems to get our attention, but even after getting our attention, He usually doesn't solve the problem immediately. He often waits for a while in order to see if we really mean business. Each of us has to answer the question, "Do I really want to change? God puts the ball in your court.

The second phase is to commit to a promise. Genesis 32:26 records an interesting turn of events in the midst of the wrestling. "Then the man said, 'Let me go, for it is daybreak.' But Jacob replied, 'I will not let you go unless you bless me.'"

Jacob did not choose to start the wrestling match. But once he was in it, he showed persistence, determination, and a resolve not to quit until he received God's blessing. He was determined that the match would not go for nothing. He basically said, "I'm committed to this struggle until I benefit from it." He made an investment of time and energy and would not give up.

Some of us have done the same thing. We have started out with a promise of something we desire, and we are willing to fight for it. There are those who have invested a lot of time and energy in their marriage and will fight to make it work. There are the students who have put hour after hour into keeping up their grades, and they are willing to fight and do whatever it takes to make it work.

Many people miss out on God's best because they give up too soon. They promise themselves and God that they will do what He wants. We desire His offer. We're such great starters, but we give up too soon. We live in a microwave society; we want instant change. "I want to pray more." Well, how much did you pray this week? "Once." Good start.

You, as Jacob did, need to determine to start where you are and go on from there. Be persistent! Heed the Lord's admonition through Paul in Galatians 6:9, "Let us not become weary in doing good, for at the proper time we will reap a harvest if we do not give up." Underline, "Don't give up!"

The third phase is to follow the process. Genesis 32:27 records a strange question from God. ". . . 'What is your name?' 'Jacob,' he answered." Had God forgotten Jacob's name? Of course not! Rather, God is using this question to lead him through a process which will make him declare who he really is—"Jacob"—which literally means "cheater." God draws on the

Jewish tradition of naming people according to what was basic to their character. For God to ask Jacob his name was to remind Jacob of all the ways he had hurt others and had brought heartbreak to many. He needed the process of coming face to face with his problem before he was willing to let God change him.

Undoubtedly, Jacob missed much of what God had for him in the first part of his life. His life was strewn with mistakes. But he didn't give up. He was humble enough that eventually he gave over the control of his life to God, even to the extent of allowing his name to be changed.

If God were to use this process on you right now, if society named you for your greatest character weakness, what would your name be? "My name is 'temperamental.'" or "My name is 'lustful.'" or "My name is 'unreliable.'" It might be "depressed" or "worrisome" or "greedy" or "resentful" or "revengeful" or any of a dozen other undesirable characteristics. Be honest. Don't mislead yourself, for the success of this process requires you to admit to yourself and then to God who you really are and what your weaknesses are. We struggle so much in our life to have a good self-image, that for some this may be a problem. True honesty with yourself can be painful, but oh so necessary to be able to make the desired changes in life and secure God's life map for the rest of your life.

The fourth phase is to apply the power that God has provided for you to live successfully your unique life map. This requires your involvement. Genesis 32:28–30 shows us how this happened for Jacob: "Then the man said, 'Your name will no longer be Jacob, but Israel, because you have struggled with God and with men and have overcome.' Jacob said, 'Please tell me your name.' But he replied, 'Why do you ask my name?' Then he blessed him there. So Jacob called the place Peniel, saying, 'It is because I saw God face to face, and yet my life was spared.'" The moment that Jacob began admitting who and what he was, he began to cooperate with God and he began to change.

Jacob had to give up his self sufficiency, admit his problem, and learn to rely upon God and His strength flowing though him. Whereas "Jacob" meant "cheater, swindler, crook," "Israel" meant "he who struggles with God" or "Prince of God." He had to be willing to give up his old identity. But what a transformation came as Jacob died to his old self, got out of the way, and let God redirect his feet onto the life map for His newly commissioned servant, "Israel"!

When God does His deepest work in our lives, it always involves the essence of who we are. Like Jacob, we need to come face to face with God's truths about us, as found in His Word. We can run from them for a while, as Jacob did until this encounter. But when we, as he, choose to give up, we then can experience God's power in us and see the changes we need. Then we, too, can have a powerful impact in our lives that will transform us from living caught in the Rat Race into experiencing a meaningful life, lived to the fullest with a life map that has us running in God's Royal Race. Our personalities will be touched and our outlook on life will be changed as God uses His transforming power flowing through us to give us an abundant and fruitful life.

Just as God knew the potential of Jacob, so He knows your potential. He created you and gifted you with specific talents so that you can follow successfully His life map for you. The choice is yours. But let me warn you, to choose not to follow God's map or to delay too long may well find you in the belly of a whale as it did for Jonah when he ran from God's revealed will. The sooner people choose to follow God's perfect plan for their lives, the more frustration and agony they can avoid and the less impact the Rat Race will have on them.

This is not to say you will have a life without problems. That is not possible or even desirable. Problems are good for us. Really they are! They help us grow. I was not half the pastor I am today just six years ago. I have matured in my preaching and counseling skills, but the maturity that really counts, the stimuli that has produced the greatest growth, are those problems which seemed unwelcome at the time. Only God knew how essential they were in shaping me, molding me and letting me be able today to help others in a much greater way.

Problems have been my friends in disguise. I am learning to thank God for them, to view new ones as ways for God to deepen my walk with Him, develop greater abilities in ministry and strengthen my ties with people as they walk through similar problems. But above all will be the fruits of righteousness that the Lord will be developing in my life, as I face these things the world calls "tragedies," "mistakes," or "impossibilities." For me, they are only more opportunities to see the goodness of the Lord, to see His faithfulness and love displayed in my life, and to experience His peace as I follow the life map He has laid out.

The final phase is to evaluate your progress. Are you where God wants you to be? Are you on target with His life map for you? Your life map serves as your plumb line for evaluation. Are you being pulled to one side or the other by even good things, that are never the less not His best for your life? Are the influences of others, the opinions of those who matter to you getting you off target and thus causing you to feel caught in the Rat Race? Go back to the plan God has given you. Search the Scriptures , and look back at the points in chapter 8. Ask the Lord to help you evaluate where you are and where He wants you to be.

My goal is never to leave His path for my life and get caught in the Rat Race again. I want to be able to say with Paul in Philippians 4:11, "I have learned to be content whatever the circumstances." My life map plays a key role in helping me safely and accurately run my race with the fewest detours and unnecessary obstacles. With my life map in place, I have a better handle on what it takes to reach God's goals for my life.

Two Important Truths

From working on my life map and helping others with theirs, I have found there are two important truths to consider. First, we must depend on God, not our own strength. Or to put it another way, will power is not enough. We all need God's power.

This was what Jacob learned when God touched his hip. Jacob was a strapping young man, full of energy and strength. When troubles came, he depended on his own strength to flee from them, his own cunning to circumvent the obstacles. But Genesis 32:31 tells us that after his all night encounter with God, "The sun rose above him as he passed Peniel, and he was limping because of his hip." God had to touch him in a corrective way at his greatest strength in order to get Jacob to stop depending on himself and start depending on God's strength. In fact, from that day forward Jacob would carry in his body the painful reminder to depend on God, and not himself. For him, running from problems was no longer an option.

God doesn't always use such drastic measures to encourage us to follow Him. It really is our decision as to how much "encouragement" God has to give. If we learn quickly from our own mistakes and from those of others that are spelled out so clearly in the Scriptures, we can avoid His having to use such dramatic steps in our lives as He did with Jacob and with Jonah. Or looking at it from another angle, the old saying is true, "The thing you resist persists." God will be faithful and persistent with us, encouraging us to seek Him for our life map no matter what condition our life currently is in. The timing for its implementation is in our hands, as is the choice to deal with the natural consequences of resisting God's leading. Personally, I want to follow my Shepherd as closely as I can, to hear only His voice, to follow only in the steps that He lays out for me. By doing these things, I avoid much of the pain the world has to offer in its Rat Race. Each day, I can meet whatever the day may hold, and know that at the end of the day I have pleased my Lord.

The second truth is not to run from personal problems. If God allows me to have a problem, I need to learn whatever lesson is there and not try to change or twist my life map to try to eliminate this problem in a wrong way. Fleeing is easy, but it is never the answer. Each problem is unique, and God alone holds the key to its solution. We need to seek His wisdom on how to handle whatever problems we are facing. Only then will we be able to grow from our experience.

Experience has taught me that when God is involved in growth or change, it lasts forever. But He leaves the choice to us. As for me, I want to run my race to win—to have completed my "map" and reached its final destination. I want to hear, "Well done, good and faithful servant" when I see God face to face. And with God's help, that is exactly what awaits me at the completion of His Royal Race for my life.

Let's go through one final series of questions to help you identify which of these five phases best describes where you are today. Have you yet recognized you have a problem? If so, are you in the second stage of committing to the struggle until God turns the burden into a blessing? Have you made it to phase three by starting to follow the process that God has put in place to help you find your life map and avoid the traps of the Rat Race? Maybe you've already moved into phase four by surrendering your own ways to God and applying His power to your life. If so, then you are in or ready to enter the continuing stage of evaluating your progress. Any road has twists and turns. Maps are not straight lines. They, too, have their areas that need constant watch, and constant adjustments in order to stay in the center of God's will. But it is a goal that you can reach with God's help. You will find Him ready and eager to help you successfully make it through your life map.

PART FOUR

Keeping the Finish Line in Sight

Chapter Thirteen

Do Less and Be More

According to an ancient tale, a man named Nasrudin had lost the key to his house. He was down on all fours under the street lamp searching frantically for his key when a stranger came along and asked him what he was looking for. Nasrudin told him that he had lost the key to his house and the stranger, being a kind man, decided to get down on his hands and knees to help look for it. After hours of searching, the stranger asked, "Are you sure you dropped the key in this spot?" Nasrudin answered, "Oh no! I dropped it way over there in that dark alley." Frustrated and angry, the stranger lost his temper, "Then why are you looking for it here?" Nasrudin replied, "Because the light's better here under the street lamp."

Those of us who are caught in the Rat Race are very much like Nasrudin. We live our supercharged lives at full throttle, focused on the external world and its perceived benefits. We fail to recognize the internal world. The Rat Race has kept us disconnected from ourselves and prevents us from knowing our potential and meaning in life as God sees us. Thus, we are defined by what we do, not by what is on the inside. The only way out of this dilemma is to redefine ourselves from within through the eyes of the Lord.

Nasrudin will find the key only if he looks in the alley where the key is. Likewise, with the Lord's help, when we look within ourselves we begin to understand what is missing and we learn to discover how to break our consistent patterns of life in the fast lane. But all too often, in our haste to have God help us solve a problem quickly, we miss getting the help that will last and remove some of the unnecessary stress of life.

David McCasland tells about a woman whose car was stalled at an intersection.

> The car's hood was up, and the woman flagged down McCasland to help. "I can't get it started," she said, "but if you jiggle the wire on the battery, I think it will work." McCasland grabbed the positive battery cable and it came off in his hand. Definitely the cable was too loose. "The terminal needs to be tightened up," he told her. "I can fix it if you have some tools." "My husband says to just jiggle the wire," she replied. "It always works. Why don't you just try that?" McCasland paused for a moment, sarcastically wondering to himself why her husband didn't ride around town with her so he would be available when the wire needed jiggling. Finally he said, "Ma'am, if I jiggle the wire, you're going to need someone else to do it every time you shut the engine off. If you'll give me two minutes and a wrench, we can solve the problem and you can forget about it." Reluctantly, she fumbled under the front seat and then extended a crescent wrench through the window of the old car. As he tightened the battery terminal, it occurred to McCasland how many times he had tried, in his own life, to get a "quick fix" from God. "I have this problem, Lord, and if You'll just jiggle the wire, things will be OK. I'm in a hurry, so let's just get me going again the quickest way possible."
>
> But God doesn't want to "jiggle wires," does He? He wants to take the time necessary to deal with our real problem and fix it. To get the long-term solution to the pressing needs in our lives requires a complete surrender to God and a willingness to proceed on His terms. We must cooperate with Him in whatever it takes, for as long as it takes. As the lady drove away with her tightened terminal, McCasland stopped for a moment and asked the Lord to say "No!" the next time he asks God to just jiggle a wire.[1]

SEARCHING IN THE WRONG PLACE

Unfortunately, we search for meaning in the "doing" side of life. We hope that when the "doing" is sufficiently fulfilling, the "being" side of life will be fulfilled as well. This is not the case. From God's perspective, we need to walk in what He has already declared us to be. Our being is centered in Him, in Christ's completed work on the cross and what transpired at the point of salvation. We not only received salvation, but we received and continue to receive much more. We receive everything that we need to walk successfully in the Christian life. We are complete in Christ and can, as we will soon learn, have all the fullness of God's Spirit indwelling us and helping us to be all God created us to be. Through God's indwelling Spirit, we can overcome the pitfalls, the detours, and the crashes that can occur in the Rat Race, and we can learn to handle and even reduce the pressures of life.

There is a book in your Bible neatly tucked away, about two-thirds, the way through the Old Testament, called the Book of Ecclesiastes. Written by a man named Solomon, it appeals to the young to heed the warnings of an older man who has grown, matured, and learned how to prepare others for the problems of life. Solomon speaks of successes and frustrations. He tells of all the ways in which he tried to make something of his life, and of all the reasons why the question, "What does it all mean in the long run?" was never really answered from a human perspective.

Like many a rich man, Solomon gave himself to pleasure, drinking, carousing, and sampling all the other distractions that money can buy. "I thought in my heart, 'Come now, I will test you with pleasure to find out what is good.' But that also proved to be meaningless. 'Laughter,' I said, 'is foolish. And what does pleasure accomplish?' . . . I denied myself nothing my eyes desired; I refused my heart no pleasure. My heart took delight in all my work, and this was the reward for all my labor. . . . Then I turned my thoughts to consider wisdom, and also madness and folly. What more can the king's successor do than what has already been done?" (Eccles. 2:1–2, 10, 12).

If there had been psychiatrists in Jerusalem twenty-five hundred years ago, Solomon might have gone to one and said, "I'm just not happy and it's all because I feel that something is missing in my life. I've tried it all. I've done it all. But, I feel like I'm wasting a lot of my time and talents. I feel like I too easily give into temptation and ignore what God expects of me. With all of the advantages I have had, where did I go wrong?"

From any good therapist, Solomon would have probably heard, "Why are you being so hard on yourself? Be realistic, lower your standards. After all, you're only human." And Solomon would have left the neat little office even more disappointed in himself, knowing this was not the advice he needed. Solomon, like so many caught in the Rat Race, had set his goals high. In order to sense meaning in life, he had to feel that he was called to do something important.

This is why Solomon in Ecclesiastes asks the question, "What makes life matter? Is there more to life than doing all you can do and than being forgotten when you are dead?" Solomon, disappointed by pleasure, wealth, and learning, tried vainly to build a foundation for his life all by himself. However, the one item he failed to include as essential is the need to recognize the significance God can play in his life.

Solomon's writings show that he greatly neglected the spiritual side of living. In his later years, Solomon explored life to its fullest in his own strength, in his own ways, giving only lip-service to God. He was out of kilter and needed balance from God. Because he ignored God's rules, he suffered the natural consequences in his own life: the consequences of emptiness, of lack of meaning in life, of everything being "vanity of vanities" as Solomon frantically filled his life with "doing." Apart from God there is no real meaning in anyone's life.

That is not to say that Solomon was ignorant of the need for God. He [God] wrote, "He has also set eternity in their heart, yet so that man will not find out the work which God has done from the beginning even to the end. I know that there is nothing better for them than to rejoice and to do good in one's lifetime; moreover that every man who eats and drinks sees good in all his labor—it is the gift of God" (Ecclesiastes 3:11–13, NASB) For Solomon to come to such a conclusion is to make a gigantic leap of faith from *doing* to *being*.

Jesus Christ lived, died, and rose from the dead to show us that the only way to have a relationship with God is through Him. John says, "Yet to all who received him, to those who believed in his name, he gave the right to become children of God" (John 1:12)

God's way of determining success is through relationship and who we are because of that relationship. This stands out in stark contrast to our best efforts at judging success. Secular society can only judge by results or by achievements. Did you win or lose? Did you succeed or fail? Did you show a profit or a loss? God alone can judge us on the basis of who we are, not what we have done. "But the Lord said to Samuel, 'Do not consider his appearance or his height, for I have rejected him. The Lord does not look at the things man looks at. Man looks at the outward appearance, but the LORD looks at the heart'" (1 Sam. 16:7).

God has built into us some basic desires, which when followed, will help us to find our self worth from being what He has created us to be. So let's look at some of the basic things humans want to be.

BASIC HUMAN "BEINGS"

Being Good. Human beings, whether they will admit it or not, have an innate need to be good. We feel uncomfortable and unfulfilled when we are not living up to our moral nature. That may be why little children who break something or do something wrong are not satisfied until they have been found out and punished; they really do not want to get away with it. They will never enjoy the idea of a good scolding or any form of discipline, but it is worse to live in a world that does not care if you do good things or bad things.

Our youngest son David will often come home from school a little on edge. He will come into the house, his face drooping, and ask, "Can I tell you something?" which means, "I did something wrong at school today, and it's driving me crazy to hold it in one moment longer, so listen up." David simply wants what we want from him—goodness.

Even some churches function in this way. The preacher may deliver "fire and brimstone" kinds of sermons, scolding the congregation for being such reprobates and sinners. This seemingly reassures the flock that God and their pastor have established high standards for them. This is a reminder to their souls of God's character and their continual need for moral sensitivity. This is part of being created in the image of God.

Being Helpful. Our human nature is such that we need to be helpful and thoughtful of the needs and concerns of others. I would contend that this is just as valuable as eating, sleeping, and exercising. When we eat too much or exercise too little, we feel out of sorts, and can forget what it's like to feel good. Likewise, helping others is a part of our nature as well, and when this core value is not allowed an opportunity to express itself, we feel empty inside.

Do you remember the story of Joseph in the Old Testament? When Joseph was seventeen, he was sold into slavery by his jealous brothers. His comfortable, secure life as "daddy's favorite" was torn away from him, leaving in its place a life filled with hardship and insecurity. For twenty years, Joseph must have dreamed of the day when he could get even with his brothers. He was willing to put up with loneliness and injustice while he anticipated, the day when his brothers would plead with him for mercy.

Then one day, it happened. Down in the land of Canaan was a famine, and Egypt was the only place that had any grain. By then Joseph had become the Pharaoh's minister of agriculture. Joseph was responsible for distributing the grain, and his brothers would soon stand before him. This was it! Joseph's big chance to get even for what they had done to him twenty years before. Joseph had ample opportunity to torment his brothers, threatening to keep them as slaves, accusing them of being spies, but something happened to Joseph. This wasn't as enjoyable as he had dreamed. He discovered that the human soul was not made for jealousy and revenge, but for helping others.

In the same way that the human body is fashioned so that eating certain foods and doing certain activities are healthy, I believe God has made us in His likeness so that certain behaviors towards other people are healthy. We literally will feel better when we have gone out of our way to be helpful to someone.

One observation, though. Some people get caught in the Rat Race by not knowing how to keep this part of their character in balance; they can overdo the fulfilling of needs. This can lead to much stress and pressure and eventual burnout if the person feels driven to fulfill the needs of everyone else. God always wants balance in our life.

Being Honest. God has given everyone a conscience. It tells us many things about how we should act even when we are not yet in relationship with God through Jesus Christ. One of these things is honesty. We want from others to be able to trust them. So our conscious then tells us that we, too, need to measure up to this standard. We choose whether or not to comply with such promptings. When we choose to go against our conscience, guilt results. This is part of being created in the image of God. The closer we draw to God, the more important honesty becomes to us and the greater our desire to be absolutely honest in every area of our life. Here are some good first steps to become honest: pay your taxes, drive the speed limit, return the books and tools you borrow.

Ask the Holy Spirit to show you other honest things to do.

Being Faithful. Being faithful cuts across the grain of a generation that rebelled. The baby boomers, the most studied generation in history, were spiritually shaken in the sixties and have become the pillars upon which social change has been built. Peter Steinfels, writing for *The New York Times* concerning Wade Clark Roof's book titled, *A Generation of Seekers* (Harper Collins, 1993), reported, "There is a kind of spiritual renewal occurring among members of this generation, but it does not necessarily mean a return to organized religion. Of the 76 million members of the baby boom generation-almost all of whom had something of a religious upbringing—Mr. Roof found a third never stopped going to church."[2]

God is faithful. He expects His children to be faithful. We see Jesus talk often about the "good and faithful servant." We expect our friends to be faithful and are deeply disappointed and hurt when they are not. The bottom line is that when we are faithful, we are more fulfilled. We have a sense of being right and having done well; our self-esteem is strengthened. Nothing can do more to undermine ourselves in our own eyes than to do something that hurts our standing in the eyes of others. God knew this and told us in Proverbs 28:20, "A faithful man will be richly blessed. . . ."

Being Compassionate. Compassion is a wonderful human quality. Those who have it are reflecting God's heart, for He is compassionate even towards those who do not deserve compassion. To be able to identify or empathize with another person's situation and to have your emotions touched with what people are feeling in their difficulties, are qualities that God has placed in our hearts.

STAYING ON TRACK

God gives us the ability to live our lives successfully and not get caught in the many traps of the Rat Race. By now you should have the confidence that this is a doable thing for your life. However, all of us need to know not only how to get on track but how to stay there. The following are important steps to apply whenever you have found yourself off track and caught in the Rat Race.

First, ask the Lord to show you where you have gotten off track. This will almost inevitably be the process that side tracked you: You will have chosen to believe a lie or a partial truth about God, another person, or yourself. Identify the lie(s) and write them down. For example, you may have been believing, *I am so far behind that I will never catch up. This is the way I have always lived my life so why bother to try to change?* These are classic Rat Race thoughts that the Enemy of your soul would love you to believe. These thoughts keep you from trying. They bring depression. Indeed, you feel trapped! There is a subtle inference here that even God cannot get you out of this mess.

Second, write down God's truth about this lie. Include any verses you know to back up this truth. In this example, you could claim Philippians 4:13 (NKJV), "I can do all things through Christ who strengthens me."

Third, admit that you've sinned as soon as you have done it, then ask for forgiveness and God's help to get back onto His path for your life. When God shows you something you've been doing that is not in His will for you, then agree with Him that it is wrong. Ask for His help not to do this again. Peter had to do this when he denied the Lord. He had been lured into sin by caving into fear and pressures. Yet as soon as he recognized his sin and confessed, he was restored to a right relationship with God. Judas refused to take this step and suffered the natural consequences of resisting restoration through confession.

So in this case you might pray, *Lord, I really feel trapped with my life out of control. I feel I can never catch up, that I'll always be in this mess. But I know that this is not the abundant life You want for me and that I've been believing a lie. I have contributed to this mess by* (name the things you've done wrong). *Please forgive me for these sins. I'm once again turning over to You every aspect of my life and asking You, Holy Spirit, to take control of my life and make it as You want it to be."*

Fourth, make things right with anyone whom you have offended. Pride is one of the strong Enemy traps in the Rat Race. It is the opposite of humility, which is God's standard. Pride can keep us from reconciliation even when we know we are wrong. Job's friends had to humble themselves and ask for him to pray for them in order to fulfill God's demands for restoration. In turn, Job had to forgive them and be willing to pray sincerely for them to be restored.

Fifth, bring every thought under the control of Jesus as we are admonished to do in 2 Corinthians 10:5. All sin starts in the mind. Therefore, keeping the mind under the control of the Lord will go a long way toward avoiding any and all traps of the Enemy. This is the principle on which Job operated. He submitted his mind to God. He asked for understanding when things seemed to be confusing or contradicting to what he understood to be God's ways. But he did not *demand* to understand before submitting to the Lord.

Sixth, ask God to show you where you are not fully trusting Him. When we are trusting God fully and following His ways, we seldom get caught in the Rat Race.

There may be several negative steps that led to your current problem. You'll need godly wisdom to know how to undo them. So when you make a mistake, you may find it helpful to ask Him to show you what led to this mistake. It may have been that you wanted your way, or that you felt your "rights" had been violated, or any number of reasons. If so, God is showing you that you fell into the trap of Satan by being self-centered. Anger and misunderstanding usually stem from self-centeredness. Pride is often involved in such problems.

What could you have done or how could you have responded differently to avoid the mistake? What warning signs do you need to be looking out for to avoid falling into the same trap again?

Seventh, list Bible verses that show you what you should do in this situation, what God's will is, and how His attributes and nature meet your need. Choose to believe what the Word says no matter what your feelings may be saying. Read the verses aloud. Use them every time you are tempted to believe Satan's lies about you, about God, or about others.

Eighth, ask the Holy Spirit to give you guidance, and to fill you and control you, especially in the area of your thoughts.

Admit your weaknesses and vulnerability. Ask Him to show you when the enemy is trying to lure you down a wrong path. Ask for His strength and courage to resist each and every opportunity to get pulled into the Rat Race or onto a detour.

Finally, refocus your mind on your original goals. Start heading for them again, and be careful not to get pulled off God's Royal Road again or in any other way, to get your focus off doing the very best in your Royal Race. Review the material in chapters 5 and 6 use it as a check list against your own life now. Make any necessary corrections. What were your original priorities? How about your current walk with the Lord compared to how it used to be? What standards have you lowered? Ask the Lord to help you be holy as He is holy.

The Rat Race is not just something the enemy has designed to keep us less effective. It really is meant to destroy or greatly damage the long term effectiveness of believers. The elements of the Rat Race that seduce a person into morally or ethically compromising situations can ruin their testimony and effectiveness for the Lord.

Applying these steps can help you reprioritize your life and avoid traps that lead to real problems, diminished potential, and possible defeat. No one is exempt from the perils of the Rat Race. But all can be victorious in the Lord.

Conclusion

So then, does it make a difference how I live? Does it make a difference if I am a good, helpful, honest, faithful, and loving person? It will not make a difference in your bank account or in your chances for fame and fortune. But sooner or later, we can learn as Solomon did, that these are the kinds of things that really matter. "Now all has been heard; here is the conclusion of the matter: Fear God and keep his commandments, for this is the whole duty of man. For God will bring every deed into judgment, including every hidden thing, whether it is good or evil," (Ecclesiastes 12:13–14)

It matters that we learn how to share our lives with others, making them and our world different because of what God is doing in us, and we are becoming. It matters if we learn to recognize that the pleasures of every day (food, work, and friendships) are simply expressions of God's presence in our lives and His wonderful desire to meet all of our needs.

I have stood at the Grand Canyon and have seen this massive gorge that has been cut by the mighty Colorado River. To the casual observer, it would seem that nothing on earth is harder than rock and nothing easier to divert than water. Yet, over the centuries, the water has won the battle, cutting into and reshaping the rock. No one drop of water is stronger than rock, but each one contributed to the ultimate victory. So it is with Christians in life. Shall we remain trapped in Rat Race thinking, wondering if we could ever have an impact or will we instead slowly seek to change our world, by stepping back and resting in the power of Almighty God, who will change us—one person at a time.

There once was a starfish that lived in the ocean. "Pardon me," he said to the whale. "Could you tell me where I can find the sea?"

"You're already in the sea," replied the whale. "Its all around you."

"This?" replied the starfish. "This is just the ocean. I'm looking for the sea."

The frustrated starfish swam away to continue searching for the sea.

"Look no further," yelled the wise old whale after him. "*Seaing* is a matter of *seeing!*"

As you make the transition in how you view your life, you will proably remain the same person on the outside. You may keep the same job and the same relationships. You may still get angry and impatient sometimes, and there may be occasions when you feel sad or disappointed. But remember, your transformation happens on the inside through God's help. You will look at your life in a different way and see things with new insight and greater clarity as God shows you His perspective and helps you keep each thought under His control.

An important truth we sometimes forget is that as part of our "being," our life is to revolve around the Lord. Unfortunately for many, when Jesus comes into their lives, they say "O.K., now my eternal destiny is taken care of, so I'll live the Christian life the best I can." We set Jesus aside as someone who can help us achieve our goals and assist us when we get into trouble. In general, He becomes our servant, rather than we His. Pascal was right. Jesus is God's solution to the vacuum in our life. But that vacuum extends far beyond the initial need for salvation; it permeates every area of our lives. This is where we often fall short, where we miss God's mark and start on a detour of life that leads straight into the Rat Race or worse.

So let's get back to basics again. Jesus needs to be at the center of our life. He needs to be integral to all we do. He, not our desires, becomes our plumb line. He sets the standards. Say it any way you wish, the bottom line is, Who is in control of your life?—you or the Lord?

When you are able to answer "the Lord," you are well on your way to being all God wants you to be and to discovering the wonderful, abundant life He has for you In so doing, you can avoid the pressures the world tries to put on you, the traps of the Enemy, and the many frustrations of the Rat Race. You will discover the joys of *being* and no longer try to *do*. *To do* is the Rat Race. *To be* is God's Royal Race. May the Lord help you stay in His race for you, so that you may be able to say with Paul in 2 Timothy 4: 7–8: "I have fought the good fight, I have finished the race, I have kept the faith. Now there is in store for me the crown of righteousness, which the Lord, the righteous Judge, will award to me on that day—and not only to me, but also to all who have longed for his appearing."

Endnotes

Chapter 1

1. "Patterns" by Paul Simon, 1965.
2. Merrill C. Tenney, ed., *The Zondervan Pictorial Bible Dictionary* (Grand Rapids, MI: Zondervan Publishing House), 589.
3. Judith Waldrop, "You'll Know It's the 21st Century When . . . ," *The Saturday Evening Post,* (April, 1991) vol. 263, no. 3: 68.
4. *The Wall Street Journal* (May 25, 1993): 3.
5. Patrick Morley, *The Man in the Mirror* (Brentwood, Tenn.: Wolgemuth & Hyatt, Publishers, Inc., 1989) [Adapted from Morley's list on p. 9].

Chapter 3

1. A term used by Church Growth expert Dr. Gary McIntosh to describe those people born prior to 1946.
2. Landon Y. Jones, "The Baby Boomers," *Money,* (vol. 12, no. 3): 300.
3. Michael P. Green, ed., *Illustrations For Biblical Preaching,* (Grand Rapids: Baker Book House,1982): 161.

Chapter 4

1. *Baby Busters* is another term for *posties.*
2. Alice Kahn and Shann Nix, "Boomers vs. Posties: Who's Stressed and Who's Blessed," *San Francisco Chronicle,* (12 July 1993): C3.
3. Max Anders, *The Good Life* (Dallas: Word Publishing, 1993), 209.
4. The term "pre-boomer" is merely a reference taken from the fact that this is the generation that preceded the baby boomers; some are now calling them "builders."

5. Doug Murren, *Baby Boomerang,* (Ventura: Regal Books,1990), 32-33.
6. "Here Come the Baby Boomers," *U.S. News & World Report* (5 November 1984) vol. 97, no. 19: 68.
7. Gary L. McIntosh, *Three Generations* (Grand Rapids, MI: Fleming H. Revell, 1995) p. 91 of written manuscript.
8. Murren, *Baby Boomerang,* 33.
9. For other interesting pieces of trivia and a real glimpse into everyday life, read *American Averages,* by Mike Feinsilber and William B. Mead, Dolphin Books, Doubleday & Company, Inc: Garden City, New York. 1980
10. Doug Sherman and William Hendricks, *Your Work Matters to God* (Colorado Springs: Nav Press, 1987), 17.
11. Earl F. Palmer, *Integrity in a World of Pretense* (Downers Grove, Ill.: Inter Varsity Press,1992), 179
12. Bill Hybels, *Who You Are When No One's Looking* (Downers Grove, Ill.: Inter Varsity Press,1987), 7–8.
13. Gordon MacDonald, *Ordering Your Private World* (Nashville: Oliver Nelson Publishers, 1984), 90.
14. E. C. McKenzie, *14,000 Quips and Quotes* (Grand Rapids: Baker Book House, 1980), 172.
15. Stephen R. Covey, *The 7 Habits of Highly Effective People* (New York: Simon and Schuster, 1989), 304.
16. Ibid, p. 306
17. NIV-Manuscript originally quoted in KJV
18. Doug Sherman, *Keeping Your Head Up When Your Job's Got You Down* (Brentwood, Tenn.: Wolgemuth & Hyatt, Publishers, Inc., 1991), 62–63.

Chapter 5

1. *The Preachers Illustration Service* (Margate: N.J.: I:2, (March 1988): 12:8.
2. Dallas Willard, *The Spirit of the Disciplines* (San Francisco: Harper Collins, 1988), 261, 262
3. I am assuming for purposes of this illustration that since the text says Jesus came to Martha's house and does not mention that it belonged to either Mary or Lazarus, that Martha was probably married as were her brother and sister, who would have each had their own home in their village of Bethany. Women married in their teens

at this time in history. The other passages mentioning Mary and Martha do not contradict my assumption. Because of their personality types, I am also assuming that Martha is the older of the two.

4. As quoted by Bill Hybles and Rob Wilkins in *Descending into Greatness,* (Grand Rapids: Zondervan Publishing House, 1993), 72–73.

Chapter 6

1. Dallas Willard, *In Search of Guidance* (Grand Rapids: Zondervan Publishing House, 1993), x.

Chapter 7

1. Adapted from Parables, Etc., 14:7:3, quoting Tom O'Keefe from an article in *Magazine Week.*
2. Willard, *In Search of Guidance*, ix.
3. Gary R. Collins, *Christian Counseling, A Comprehensive Guide* (Waco: Word Books, 1980), 84.
4. Robert Hemfelt, Frank Minirth, Paul Meier, Deborah Newman, and Brian Newman, *Love Is a Choice Workbook* (Nashville: Thomas Nelson Publishers, 1991), 4–5.

Chapter 8

1. Adapted from *The Rhythm of Life* by Richard Exley as published in Parables, Etc., January 1991, page 7.
2. Green, ed., *Illustrations for Biblical Preaching*, 377.
3. Steven Douglass, *Enjoying Your Walk with God* (San Bernardino: Here's Life Publishers, 1989), 93
4. Chuck Swindoll, *Flying Close to the Flame* (Dallas: Word Publishing, 1993), 75.
5. Ibid., 77–78.
6. Charles Stanley, *The Wonderful Spirit-Filled Life* (Nashville: Oliver Nelson Books, 1992), 11.

Chapter 10

1. William Hendriksen, *New Testament Commentary,* "Luke," (Grand Rapids: Baker Book House, 1978), 291.

Chapter 11

1.   C. F. Keil and F. Delitzsch, *Commentary on the Old Testament, Volume II, Joshua, Judges, Ruth, I & II Samuel* (Grand Rapids: William B. Eerdmans Publishing Co., 1984), 187.
2.   Pat Riley, "What Winners Know," *Reader's Digest* (March 1994): 144:863:176. Condensed from *The Winner Within* (New York: G. P. Putnam's Sons, 1993).
3.   Horace L. Fenton Jr., *When Christians Clash* (Downers Grove, Ill.: InterVarsity Press, 1987), 38-39
4.   Tim Hansel, *When I Relax I Feel Guilty* (Weston,. Ontraio: David C. Cook Publishing Co., 1981), 68.
5.   Ibid., 2.
6.   Archibald Hart, *Adrenaline and Stress* (Waco, Texas: Word Books, 1986), 167

Chapter 12

1.   Nate Adams, *Energizers,* Campus Life Books (Grand Rapids: Zondervan Publishing House, 1994), 15–16.
2.   Gary L. McIntosh, "Ministry in the Information Age, Part 1," *The McIntosh Church Growth Network,* 1:8 (Aug. 1989): 1–2.
3.   Submitted by Billy D. Strayhorn, Parables, Etc. 13:12:3, February, 1994.
4.   Bill Bright, *The Holy Spirit* (San Bernardino: Here's Life Publishers, 1980), 233.
5.   Larry Gilbert, *Team Ministry: A Guide to Spiritual Gifts and Lay Involvement* (Church Growth Institute, P.O. Box 4404, Lynchburg, VA 24502), 1987.

Chapter 13

1.   "One to Grow On," Power For Living, S.P. Pub. Inc. 10-9-88. Contributed by Rev. Wayne Rouse.
2.   Peter Steinfels, "Charting the Currents of Belief For the Generation That Rebelled," *The New York Times,* Sunday, (30 May 1993), E-1.